The Remedial Teacher's Handbook

P. S. Westwood M.Ed., L.C.P., M.A.P.S.

'Though slow learners and the socially disadvantaged
often appear to have less to offer, this is a measure
of their need rather than an indication of their limits.' R. GULLIFORD

(*Backwardness and Educational Failure*, 1969, Slough, N.F.E.R. p. 48)

Oliver & Boyd

Oliver & Boyd
Robert Stevenson House
1–3 Baxter's Place
Leith Walk
Edinburgh EH1 3BB

A Division of Longman Group Ltd.

© Peter Westwood 1975

ISBN 05 002852 9

Reprinted 1976, 1977, 1978, 1979 (updated)

Printed in Hong Kong by
Wah Cheong Printing press Ltd

Contents

Contents

Introduction

The entire philosophy behind this book is epitomised in the statement by Tina Bangs in *Language and learning disorders of the pre-academic child* (1968, Appleton-Century-Crofts):

Children make better use of their potential when learning is not left to chance.

In other words this is a book written for the teacher who believes in *systematic teaching*: it attempts to provide practical advice throughout.

Recognising the fact that remedial teachers are still primarily concerned with the teaching of language arts to slow learners, main emphasis has been placed upon the evaluation and structured teaching of language skills including, of course, reading. Rather less has been provided on number and mathematics. Attention to important matters of organisation has been given in the final sections.

This book does not set out to discuss in detail the aetiology of various forms of learning disability; not because this isn't important, but because it has been done very thoroughly already by several authors, in particular Gulliford in *Backwardness and Educational Failure* (1969, N.F.E.R.) and *Special Educational Needs* (1971, Routledge) and Francis-Williams in *Children with Specific Learning Difficulties* (1970, Pergamon).

The early sections of the book deal with diagnosis and assessment. It should be pointed out that even the most sophisticated diagnostic test cannot always prove conclusively the basic *cause* of a child's learning problems. Rather than seeking some subtle specific cause while carrying out in-depth assessment of a child's difficulties, it is more useful to consider the stages of development already reached by the child, the skills he has already mastered, and the implications from these for the next step in teaching that child.

This book is aimed at teachers following initial, in-service, and more advanced courses of training in special education. Teachers in initial training are also advised to read at least one of the following books before working through this Handbook:

BELL, P. *Basic Teaching for Slow Learners* (1970, Muller).
HAIGH, G. *Teaching Slow Learners* (1977, Temple Smith).
WILLIAMS, A. A. *Basic Subjects for the Slow Learner* (1970, Methuen).

The author wishes to acknowledge with gratitude the help given by the following: Gerry Lucas, Mike Hughes, Joyce Nolan, and Kath Scrymgeour in the standardisation of the two arithmetic tests which appear in Chapter 6; Mr. E. Shearer, Senior Educational Psychologist for Cheshire for permission to reproduce the new norms for the Burt-Vernon *Graded Word Reading Test* in Appendix 2; and Miss I. Whitehill and Mrs. J. Nolan for permission to reproduce samples of work from adults/adolescents with problems of literacy.

Peter Westwood.
Stockport 1974.

1. The early identification of learning difficulties: nursery and infant stages

Those who are engaged in the education of slow learning children are becoming increasingly aware of the fact that such children's progress depends not merely on the therapeutic measures when failure has been established but on the early detection and consequent preventive strategies.[9]

Almost all of the children who will ultimately be destined for placement in schools or units for the mentally subnormal, the blind, the deaf and the physically handicapped will have been recognised during the pre-school period. The increasing use of 'at risk' registers, for example, has meant that such pupils can be followed up and the assessment of needs carried out and reviewed regularly. However, it is regrettable that it still remains fairly typical of the borderline educationally subnormal child, the slow learner, and the child with specific learning disabilities that they will need to show themselves as failures within the ordinary school setting before action is taken.

The number involved is not small. We are faced with the probability that at least 13% to 16% of pupils in 'average' infant schools require some form of special help for some part of their early primary schooling.[10] [11] [16] In some depressed areas, particularly the urban slums and over-spill estates where the child population is known to be 'educationally at risk',[17] the figure 16% is a gross underestimation of the extent of the need. Failure to provide adequate special help at primary level undoubtedly goes a long way towards explaining the fact that, at secondary school level, it is not at all uncommon to find more than 20% of the pupils needing special educational help.[4]

It is obvious that children with potential learning difficulties do need to be identified at the earliest possible moment, ideally before they have to experience prolonged periods of educational failure. Such early identification should fulfil a preventive function and thus minimise the need later for what is commonly known as 'remedial education'.

This line of thought has resulted in an increasing number of local education authorities introducing screening procedures to identify 'at risk' pupils at the infant level. It has also resulted in educational researchers giving some attention to the development

1

of suitable batteries of tests and assessment schedules to facilitate such screening.

The identification of pupils with special needs will not necessarily result in their being removed from the normal school setting. It will always be appropriate and desirable for the majority of such children to remain in the ordinary school and receive additional help there. In some cases the child's needs can be met adequately within the ordinary classroom, perhaps by delaying his introduction to such 'formal' skills as reading and writing while suitable training activities are provided to bring him as quickly as possible to a state of readiness for such teaching. Sometimes the special help will mean nothing more than a modification of usual teaching methods or materials in order to overcome or compensate for some particular weakness which the child exhibits. In other circumstances, it may be more useful to place the child in a special group for part or all of the day. One can then meet his needs most successfully by adapting the whole of the curriculum to deal with the special problems. Matters of organisation, methods, and materials are dealt with later in the book.

Teachers in charge of nursery and infant classes should play a key role in the detection of children with special needs. There is evidence that their subjective assessments can be very accurate and perceptive.[38][14] An experienced teacher, acquainted with normal child development, is in an excellent position to observe deviations in individual cases.

Teachers tend to rate children with learning difficulties as less mature, less ready for academic work, having poor attention span, being poor at art work, having poor motor control, poor social and emotional adjustment, poor speech and language, and being more impulsive in their behaviour. However, all these traits or symptoms do not necessarily occur together in an individual child; nor is it found that these weaknesses are entirely absent in children who make good progress in school.[3] It needs to be stressed that there is normally a wide range of performance and development levels in young children, and a teacher should not attach undue importance to isolated areas of weakness, particularly where these do not appear to be impeding educational progress. It is when a number of these symptoms cluster together that the indications begin to gain weight.

Following a six-year study of infants with special needs, Webb concluded that identification of such children is perhaps easier in a classroom situation where the regime is reasonably relaxed and informal. 'Under such circumstances it is possible for children to express their fears and needs more readily than if teachers are afraid of their own feelings, rigid in approach, and over-formal in teaching methods' (p. 23).[16] She also stresses the importance of record keeping by the class teacher; not merely noting the reading book and page number a child may be on, or the particular aspect of number work being covered (although these are important), but commenting upon the child's attitudes to work, home background, social adjustment, deviant behaviour, etc. Such recording, over a period of time, may present a consistent pattern which has been overlooked while dealing with isolated incidents week by week.

Observation of behaviour needs to be reasonably objective. Teachers' assessments, valuable as they are, inevitably tend to be subjective and generalised; they may identify the children in need but not produce specific information with direct implications for teaching and planned intervention. It is in this direction that teachers require most help.

In general there is fair agreement concerning the relevant skills and behaviours to observe. Edwards[5] suggests that teachers of very young children watch for the following prognostic signs of possible learning difficulties: (i) child spends most of his/her time on tasks requiring minimal intellectual effort (e.g. pushing dolls pram, playing with sand); (ii) generally poor performance in most activities attempted; (iii) short span of attention; (iv) poor understanding of stories read to group; (v) difficulty in co-ordinating movements, poor at tasks requiring hand-eye co-ordination and spatial judgement (inset form-boards, filling in colours, cutting with scissors, building with bricks); (vi) difficulty in learning simple songs and following instructions; (vii) inability to remember where to find toys or apparatus in the room; (viii) very immature articulation; (ix) limited vocabulary; (x) hyperactivity; (xi) withdrawal from interpersonal contacts; (xii) low threshold of frustration, over-aggressive, disruptive; (xiii) in the case of the slow learner, lack of recognisable improvement with the passage of time. (Edwards points out that children who are culturally deprived pre-school but otherwise free from handicap *do* tend to show marked improvement.)

Very similar summaries of important areas for observation of young children are provided by Francis-Williams[7] and Banks.[1]

Some investigators have attempted to remove at least part of the subjective element in teacher observation through the use of specific tests for which norms are available or for which rating scales can be employed.[6][8][14][15] Unfortunately, several of the tests which are frequently selected by the researcher are not available for general classroom use. One of the best known studies of this kind was that reported by de Hirsch and her colleagues in 1966.[8] They set out to find the best group of tests or assessments to use with children in the age range five to six and a half years in order to identify the children most likely to experience difficulty in learning to read, write, and spell. Initially 37 sub-tests were used, plus information about the child's background and pre-school experience. Finally, a battery of ten tests was selected as providing the best set of predictors, and a scoring system was devised. The assessments remaining in de Hirsch's 'predictive index' covered: grasp of pencil, copying of shapes, auditory discrimination, verbal output, knowledge of 'category' words, visual discrimination of word shapes, tendency to reverse shapes, and three tasks of immediate learning and recall using flashcards. Unfortunately, the index necessitates the use of the *Visual-motor Gestalt test*, Holst's *Reversal test*, Wepman's *Auditory discrimination test*, and a sub-test from Gate's *Reading readiness test*: none of these are readily available to class teachers.

More recently, Meyers, Ball, and Crutchfield[13] used the de Hirsch battery as a starting point for the development of their *Kindergarten testing procedure*, a particularly promising instrument when used with selected pupils who have first been identified by more subjective means. Their final schedule covers: (i) the copying of shapes; (ii) reproduction of the same shapes from memory; (iii) drawing of the human figure; (iv) identification of parts of own body; (v) the imitation of movements made by examiner; (vi) hopping, skipping, walking a line, catching; (vii) bead stringing (with time limit); (viii) hand preference; (ix) auditory discrimination; (x) understanding of language patterns and vocabulary; (xi) a consideration of behaviour patterns (hyperactivity, distractibility, impulsivity, immaturity, etc.). This kind of in-depth evaluation leads directly to implications for teaching; and specific suggestions are contained in their handbook, which is recommended reading for teachers working with young handicapped children.[13]

In this country the *Swansea infant evaluation profiles*[15] use information from home background, medical history and adjustment to school, together with results from tests of vocabulary, visual perception, hand-eye co-ordination, basic number concepts and the ability to carry out an immediate learning task using symbols. A scoring system is used and an 'at risk' score determined in individual cases.

Jones[9] recommends the use of a fairly simple developmental profile for the infant. This is to be completed by the teacher using a five-point rating scale for eleven aspects of development: (i) physical growth and development; (ii) motor control; (iii) visuo-motor co-ordination; (iv) visual perception; (v) auditory perception; (vi) intelligence; (vii) language development; (viii) reading; (ix) number; (x) emotional development; (xi) social development. Obvious areas of weakness would then appear as low points on the profile and therefore demand attention.

In America the *First grade screening test* devised by Pate and Webb[14] represents one of the few attempts to confine the assessment procedure to a paper-and-pencil type test capable of administration to groups. The assessments made within the test booklet cover drawing of human figure, copying of square and diamond, control of pencil, following oral instructions, understanding of vocabulary, comprehension from pictures, short-term recall of picture material, perception of self and parent figures. This test is available in Britain from Education Evaluation Enterprises, Bristol.

Mention has already been made of the importance of socio-cultural disadvantage as an important predictor of possible learning difficulties. This probably remains the best single indicator of a possible need for special help in the early stages of schooling.

Another important factor, but one not so readily identified, is the pre-school history of difficult pregnancy, difficult birth, or abnormal early developmental pattern. It should not be inferred that abnormal pregnancy, difficult or premature birth, and late attainment of the important pre-school developmental milestones of sitting, walking, feeding, and speech development, automatically predispose a child to learning difficulties at school. But abundant evidence exists to show that such conditions are not infrequently associated with later perceptual or behavioural disorders and learning problems.[2 7 8 12] Knowledge of such early history could be useful as a first indicator, and yet it is rarely asked for from a parent when a child is first presented for school.

The schedule which follows is designed to direct the attention of teachers to important facets of background, behaviour and skills which are relevant. Clearly the importance of each of the factors, particularly in section B, is relative to the child's chronological age. It is necessary to repeat that only when a number of these adverse pointers occur together do the implications gain weight.

The schedule may be reproduced without infringing copyright.

Observation schedule

PREDICTORS OF POSSIBLE LEARNING DIFFICULTIES

A Background information

1. Is the child from a culturally deprived/socially disadvantaged background?
2. Does he/she come from a 'pathological' or 'problem' family?
3. Are the parents' own educational standards very low?
4. Are the parents' levels of expectation for the child unreasonably high?
5. Has the child any known handicaps or defects?
6. Have brothers/sisters exhibited retardation and learning problems?
7. Did brothers/sisters have poor attendance records?
8. Do the parents express any worries concerning some aspect of the child's pre-school development?
9. Was the child's birth difficult? Were there complications? Was he/she very under-weight/premature?
10. Did the child reach the developmental milestones of walking and talking at the normal times? (Walking unaided by 18 months. Talking intelligibly in simple terms by 2 years, and understanding much of what is said to him/her in simple terms. Lack of intelligible speech by 2½–3 years becomes significant.)

B Observations of behaviour and performance in the classroom

I *General behavioural characteristics*

1. Does he/she appear very babyish and immature in general?
2. Has he/she adjusted to the normal routine of school life?
3. Does he/she appear unhappy at school? Does he/she cry frequently?

4. Is the child abnormally aggressive and/or disruptive?
5. Is the child unusually shy and withdrawn?
6. Does he/she avoid tasks which require intellectual effort?
7. Is he/she capable of concentrating upon one task for any length of time?
8. Is the child highly distractible? Is he/she hyperactive?
9. In work or play with others is he/she capable of awaiting his/her turn?
10. During the course of the average day does he/she produce any recognisable work output?

II *Language*

1. Does he/she appear to listen and respond to instructions from the teacher?
2. Does he/she make much use of speech to communicate with adults or peers?
3. Is his/her articulation very immature, his/her utterances unintelligible, or his/her language structure very babyish?
4. Does he/she listen when a story is read or told?
5. Can he/she point to common objects named in a picture?
6. Does his/her vocabulary appear very restricted?
7. Can he/she answer simple questions about himself/herself?
8. Does he/she appear to have a possible *hearing* problem?

III *Movement, perceptuo-motor skills and memory*

1. Can he/she dress unaided? Put on shoes? Do up buttons?
2. Is he/she consistent in choice of hand for carrying out manual tasks?
3. Can he/she easily cross the 'mid-line' of the body in performing movements?
4. Is he/she markedly clumsy? In P.E. lessons does he/she lack co-ordination, balance and rhythm?
5. Can he/she use scissors for simple cutting tasks?
6. Can he/she hold a drawing or writing instrument reasonably correctly?
7. Can he/she colour in shapes with reasonable accuracy?
8. Is his/her free drawing still at a scribble stage?
9. Can he/she produce a recognisable drawing of the human figure? (Beware of regarding this as a test of *intelligence*.)

10. Can he/she copy the following shapes with reasonable accuracy? Each figure is presented on a separate card 12 cm × 10 cm. Figures should reasonably fill the card and not be too small. The ages below each figure indicate the age by which most children can copy the shape correctly.

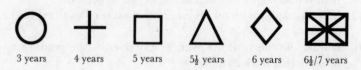

| 3 years | 4 years | 5 years | 5½ years | 6 years | 6½/7 years |

11. Can he/she complete simple inset form-boards and simple jigsaw puzzles?
12. In copying figures or letters does he/she frequently produce a *reversed* form?
13. In sorting and matching activities does he/she frequently confuse 'reversible' shapes?
14. Does he/she know the names of the basic colours?
15. Can he/she learn and retain simple units of instruction for immediate recall (e.g. two words taught from flashcards)?
16. Can he/she retain material taught from one day to the next?
17. Can he/she repeat in correct sequence the words within simple sentences said to him/her? (e.g. 'It is raining today.' 'I like this big toy.')
18. Can he/she repeat up to three numbers said to him/her? (e.g. 3–7–1.)

Suggestions for further study

(a) Use the schedule presented above for the observation of two young children, one considered by the teacher to be 'advanced' and the other 'retarded' in development and progress. How many of the adverse pointers on the schedule are apparent in the 'advanced' child also? What are your conclusions?
(b) Consider the items in the schedule, and through discussion with other teachers determine which of the possible combinations of factors might have maximum weight in predisposing a child to learning difficulties.
(c) Record keeping is considered an important part of a teacher's duties. Design a cumulative record card or sheet which would

be appropriate for systematic observation of a young child's all-round development. Remember, it should require the minimum of *writing* on the part of the teacher, but should convey the maximum amount of useful information.

References

1. BANKS, E. M. (1970) 'The identification of children with potential learning disabilities' *The Slow Learning Child*, **17**, 27–38, University of Queensland.
2. BUTLER, N. (1968) 'Growth and development of Britain's seven year olds' in *The child and the outside world*. Association for Special Education.
3. COWGILL, M., FRIELAND, S. and SHAPIRO, R. (1973) 'Predicting learning disabilities from kindergarten reports' *Jnl. Learning Disabilities*, **6**, 50–5.
4. Department of Education and Science (1971) *Slow learners in the secondary schools: Ed. survey 15*, London, H.M.S.O.
5. EDWARDS, E. (1972) 'Planning for the child who needs special understanding' *Australian Pre-School Qtly*, **13**, 8–11.
6. EVANS, J. S. and BANGS, T. (1972) 'Effects of pre-school language training on later academic achievement of children with language and learning disabilities' *Jnl. of Learning Disabilities*, **5**, 585–92.
7. FRANCIS-WILLIAMS, J. (1970) *Children with specific learning difficulties*, Oxford, Pergamon Press.
8. DE HIRSCH, K., JANSKY, J. and LANGFORD, W. (1966) *Predicting reading failure*, New York, Harper & Row.
9. JONES, H. (1971) 'Procedures for detecting children in need of special help' *Remedial Education*, **6**, No. 1, 28–30.
10. KELLMER-PRINGLE, M., BUTLER, N. and DAVIE, R. (1967) *11,000 Seven Year Olds*, London, Longman.
11. McCLELLAN, G. (1970) 'Children at risk' *The slow learning child*, **17**, 3–7, University of Queensland.
12. McDONALD, A. (1967) *Children of very low birth weight*, London, Heinemann.
13. MEYERS, E., BALL, H. and CRUTCHFIELD, M. (1973) *The Kindergarten teacher's handbook*, Los Angles, Gramercy Press.
14. PATE, J. and WEBB, W. (1969) *First grade screening test: manual*, American Guidance Service Inc. (Education Evaluation Enterprises, Bristol).
15. Schools Council Research and Development Project in Compensatory Education (1971) *Swansea infant evaluation profiles*, Swansea, University College.
16. WEBB, L. (1967) *Children with special needs in the infant school*, London, Collins (Fontana Books).
17. WIDLAKE, P. and BELL, L. (1973) *The education of the socially handicapped child*, London, Nelson & Son.

Recommended reading

DAVIE, R., BUTLER, N. and GOLDSTEIN, H. (1972) *From birth to seven*, London, Longman.
Department of Education and Science (1964) *Slow learners at school: Ed. pamphlet 46* (esp. Ch. 1, 2 and Appendix), London, H.M.S.O.
GULLIFORD, R. (1969) *Backwardness and educational failure*, Slough, N.F.E.R.
ILG, F. and AMES, L. (1965) *School readiness*, London and New York, Harper and Row.
WEBB, L. (1967) *Children with special needs in the infant school*, London, Collins.

More advanced

Francis-Williams, J. (1970) *Children with specific learning difficulties* (esp. Ch. 3, 4, 5), Oxford, Pergamon Press.

McCarthy, J. J. and McCarthy, J. F. (1969) *Learning disabilities* (esp. Ch. 1, 2, 3), Boston, Allyn and Bacon.

2. The uses and abuses of standardised tests in the identification of children with learning difficulties

Basic teacher-training courses tend to pay scant attention to the uses of tests in the classroom, in spite of the fact that testing and assessment are essential ingredients of educational practice.[12]

It may be argued that the use of standardised* tests to identify children with learning difficulties in junior, middle, or upper schools is unnecessary since the evidence of the general failure of such children is only too obvious to all concerned, and is frequently accompanied by secondary behaviour and emotional problems. To some extent this is true. Teachers do know their children, and do recognise those who are experiencing difficulties. However, this very subjective observation does not allow a particular child to be compared with others of his age who are making normal progress in order to determine the extent of his backwardness. It says nothing of the child's general mental ability, nor does it enable teachers in some situations to compare a particular child's performance across a range of subjects or skills—to note *intra-individual* differences in attainment. For example, it is all too easy for an older child, taught in a subject-specialisation situation to be judged 'dull' by a teacher simply because he is weak in a particular subject, or his spelling is poor, his handwriting untidy or his reading below average; the bright child with specific learning problems is particularly at risk in this situation. The judicious use of appropriate tests can be extremely valuable; and the results do provide information not otherwise available to the teacher. Some important points concerning interpretation and misinterpretation of test results will be presented later in this section.

The idea of educational screening is not new; and screening tests and surveys have become quite fashionable.[1] Sometimes these are carried out to assess, for example, the current national standards of reading. At other times (and more frequently), they are used to ascertain the size of the problem within a particular district or school,

* A *standardised* test is one which has been applied previously to large representative samples of children, thus providing norms against which a child may be compared. Standardisation will have ensured that the test is valid and reliable.

11

and to detect the children most in need of special help and individual follow-up.[110]

Young[18] states, 'Testing is of little use unless it helps towards decision and action' (p. 12). This point cannot be over-stressed and is worth keeping in mind throughout the following sections on attainment and diagnostic testing.

Standardised attainment tests

Attainment tests may be used to determine a child's present functional level in a particular subject (e.g. reading, spelling, mathematics). The test result enables the teacher to compare the child's performance with that of other 'typical' children used in the standardisation sample.

Attainment tests are designed either for group administration or for individual application. They tend to be of limited *diagnostic* value since this is not their purpose; but it is useful to study the nature of a child's errors revealed within his test performance, particularly in the areas of reading, spelling, and mathematics. The errors will give some indication of the precise point of failure, and will sometimes provide the first tentative insights into a child's specific difficulties.

The result from an attainment test may also give some indication of the most suitable teaching material and the correct level of difficulty at which to use it with the child.

Results from attainment tests are expressed in different ways; usually as *standardised scores,* or in terms of *percentiles,* or as *quotients,* or directly as *attainment ages.*

Standardised scores. These are not the actual total marks (raw score) obtained on the test items, but are those marks related to a common scale. Most tests are designed to provide a scale yielding a standard score of 100 as the 'mean' or average for a specified age group. Just over two thirds of the age group will get scores within 15 points above or below this mean of 100. Standardised scores permit comparison to be made directly between test results based on the same scale for the same age group.

Percentiles. Results expressed as percentiles allow a child's performance to be compared with other children in his age group, but only lead to such conclusions as, 'He is better than 75% of the age group', or 'Only 25% of the age group would have scored higher than his result'. Percentiles may be converted to standard scores by consulting an appropriate conversion table.

For a full discussion covering standard scores and percentiles see Labon,[6] Jackson,[4] or the N.F.E.R. booklet *Tests for guidance and assessment*.[19]

Quotients. A child's attainment age expressed as a percentage of his chronological age is referred to as a quotient, i.e.,

$$\frac{\text{Reading age}}{\text{Chronological Age}} \times 100 = \text{Reading Quotient.}$$

Attainment age. This indicates the typical performance of a child of a stated age; for instance, a child obtaining a spelling age of 6·5 years is performing at the level of an average six-and-a-half year-old regardless of his own age which may be well above this. Although the National Foundation for Educational Research (NFER) regards an attainment age as less meaningful than a standardised score, it is likely that a performance expressed as an age level will continue to convey more meaning to a teacher. The knowledge that a child is nine years old but reading at the level of an average six year-old is more likely to induce a teacher to take action than the same result expressed as a percentile or standardised score, both of which are frequently misunderstood and thought to imply some permanent characteristic of the child unlikely to be altered or improved.

Group testing

Group testing for screening purposes within a class can be very useful, even though the results from such tests are likely to be less accurate than those obtained from a carefully administered individual test. The main advantage of group testing is that it is economical of time. If the immediate need is to obtain a rough indication of the spread of ability, and to discover those children requiring a more searching individual assessment, it seems foolish in the extreme to spend valuable time testing each child separately as a matter of routine. This routine has been known to occupy one teacher for three weeks in a large secondary school!

In testing groups of children the following points need to be borne in mind:

(i) Schonell [12] recommended 'friendly contact', 'an element of humour', and the use of 'encouragement and praise' in dealing with testing situations. Good advice. There is no reason why children should not have enjoyed the experience if presented well.

(ii) It is as well to have tried out the test with a small group, or even with one child, before using it with a large group. In this way any minor snags in procedure will be detected.

(iii) Group testing of infants, or children with very limited ability and poor attention span, can be difficult. It is usually unwise to attempt this unless the teacher is also a skilled and experienced tester.

(iv) Groups should not be too large for testing, preferably not above twenty, and less if the children are young or of limited ability.

(v) Children must be seated in such a way that copying from a neighbour is impossible.

(vi) It is essential that the teacher follow exactly the instructions set out for the administration of the test. This applies particularly to the exact wording of directions given to the children and, where appropriate, to the observing of stated time limits. There is a marked tendency for class teachers to *want the children to do well* and, almost unconsciously, to give more help than they should. Sometimes a tendency to be unduly lenient in the marking also stems from the same motive; and the leniency appears to favour the pupils already subjectively regarded as 'good' by the teacher. This is not to suggest that the teacher should not be on the look out for a child who does perform atypically in a group testing situation. In cases of doubt an individual test should be given.

(vii) Tests should at all times be given on the correct answer sheets or booklets. To reproduce a test on a spirit or ink duplicator usually results in type of a different size or inferior form of illustration. To reproduce by photocopying almost always infringes copyright.

(viii) The giving of a group test to children outside the age range for which it was designed is of little value. The extrapolation of scores beyond the figures given in tables of norms can be extremely inaccurate. (The only possible exception to this rule is when a group test is given mainly to obtain diagnostic information rather than yield an attainment age for children in the group.)

(ix) Probably the most serious abuse of test results comes from a gross misunderstanding of what the actual figures reveal about the child's performance, his needs and his potential. For example, teachers are frequently very concerned when the results from one reading test do not match up identically with results from another reading test given soon afterwards. It is necessary to recognise that in many cases different tests yield somewhat different equivalent ages. This is to be expected; reading tests have been standardised at different times on different samples of children, and norms do alter with time. Also, one test may be sampling reading skill in a rather different way from another; one may use isolated word lists while another uses a meaningful prose passage or sentence completion items. A child may be quite skilled 'guessing within the context' of a story or sentence but may be poor at tackling an unfamiliar word in isolation. One test may slightly favour the child who has developed some phonic skill at the expense of the child who lacks this experience.

Teachers also attach too much importance to reading ages in the early stages of reading development. This point will be developed in the section on diagnosis, but it is important to realise here that a reading age of anything below five and a half to six years has little meaning. With reading ages above this one should be more concerned with the underlying skills which are present or absent than with the global description 'reading age 7·4 years'.

In particular, one needs to exercise caution in comparing a child's reading age with his spelling age, or his reading comprehension age with his reading accuracy age, and deciding that one is significantly lower than the other. If the difference is no more than a few points it is just as likely to have occurred as the result of errors of measurement or through comparing norms from quite different populations. Comparing performance levels across a variety of tests is a useful exercise; but only really marked discrepancies between levels should be regarded as probably reflecting an area of specific weakness.

Misinterpretation of test results applies particularly to measures of intelligence or mental ability. This point is made explicit below.

(x) Finally, in selecting a test for a particular group it is useful if the ages of the children fall somewhere around the middle range of the test. Most tests tend to be rather inaccurate at their upper and lower limits, and the choice of an inappropriate test can result in many of the children scoring at or near the ceiling of the test items, or, at the other extreme, failing to score at all on a test which begins at a level which is already too difficult for them.

Testing intelligence or mental ability

Teachers using tests which purport to measure intelligence should consider the following points:

(i) The notion that what is measured by a simple intelligence test is some innately determined and quite unchangeable characteristic of the child is no longer tenable.[3 5] What is measured by an intelligence test is merely the child's present functional level in the particular tasks contained in that test; his ability to process that type of information; a tiny sample of intelligent behaviour. It is at best a coarse assessment. The functional level of a child's intelligence may certainly be influenced by outside intervention.

(ii) Some measures of intelligence (those which assess verbal rather than non-verbal abilities) are likely to be better predictors of school potential.[15] The ability to deal with, or process, language remains the most important ability to possess in school situations.

(iii) The problem of testing the intelligence of children who are very backward in reading (or are non-readers) very frequently leads a teacher to administer a non-verbal reasoning test (for example, picture tests involving a minimum of verbal instruction). Single measures of non-verbal intelligence may be very misleading if taken as indicative of a child's general mental ability. Many very backward readers are average or above average in non-verbal or performance tasks. Comparisons made between, for example, reading age from a standardised reading test and mental age from a non-verbal intelligence test are virtually meaningless.

Suitable tests for assessing verbal abilities in children are presented later in this section.

While the matter of remedial help being all about 'getting a child's reading and number ages in line with his mental age' is quite rightly being seriously challenged[4 6 9 17]—and as Phillips[9] points out, '... the value of intelligence tests as predictors of response to remedial teaching of the basic education skills is negligible' (p. 72)—it is still generally agreed that some measure of a child's general intellectual abilities is worth obtaining. To some extent it is one of the factors which will determine the nature of the special help a child will receive, either *Adaptive education*, with almost all aspects of the curriculum made 'special' to meet his needs, *Compensatory education* designed to overcome various environmentally created deficiencies in the child's development, or *Remedial education* planned to help the child with particular learning difficulties within certain skill areas. Yet another sub-division is, of course, *Therapeutic education* designed to alleviate some of the emotional and behavioural problems associated with educational failure. These four sub-divisions of *Special education* should all be available within the ordinary school setting; and in many cases children with learning difficulties will require a combination of the separate forms of special help. For example, the highly intelligent child with specific learning problems will need remedial education plus therapeutic help. If he also comes from a very poor home background part of his programme is likely to be compensatory. Adaptive education is usually required for the child of limited intellectual abilities, and, in many cases, will be combined with compensatory education.

In the past the ugly question has been asked, 'Which of the failing children in this school shall we select for special help?' And the answer is still given in some areas, 'Those who will make most rapid progress as indicated by their intelligence level and attitude to work'. The procedure of selecting pupils for special help by comparing attainment age in reading with mental age from an intelligence test has been reviewed critically by Lytton.[7] Sometimes this relationship has been expressed as an 'achievement quotient' and those children selected who had achievement quotients below a certain figure. A more complicated procedure for assessing educational retardation using multiple regression equations has been outlined by Savage.[11] In all procedures using statistical or quasi-statistical methods to select some children and reject others there is an underlying assumption that we are not really going to meet individual needs in all cases. The philosophy behind this book is that *any* child who is experiencing learning difficulties should receive special help.

Tests recommended for group screening or assessment

(See Appendix for publishers'/suppliers' addresses)

1. *The non-reader's intelligence test* D. Young (University of London Press)
   One of the few tests which involves verbal reasoning and interpretation of verbal instructions but does not require reading ability. The test is untimed and is orally administered. The sub-tests are enjoyed by most children if presented as 'puzzles'.

The material can be used with children who *can* read, in which case it is advisable to cut the title of the test from the answer sheets before distribution.

Age range 6 years 7 months to 8 years 11 months for full range of intelligence. Also suitable for slow learning children up to 13 years 11 months.

Coefficient of reliability: ·95*.

Order Manual, marking template, and answer sheets.

2. *The oral verbal intelligence test* D. Young (University of London Press)

A more difficult version of the test described above.

Age range 7 years 6 months to 10 years 11 months for full range of intelligence. Also suitable for slow learners up to age 14 years 11 months.

Order Manual, marking template, and answer sheets.

3. *The English picture vocabulary tests* M. Brimer and L. Dunn (Educational Evaluation Enterprises)

These tests assess receptive or listening vocabulary of the children. They do not require a spoken response, the child merely marks the appropriate picture to denote a word spoken by the examiner.

The English picture vocabulary tests (*EPVT*) have been found useful for detecting slow learning juniors, particularly those whose difficulties stem mainly from a very restricted experience of language.[8] Tests 1 and Pre-school can only be administered to individual children, but Test 2 and Test 3 are designed for group administration.

Age range Pre-school   3 years to 4 years 11 months.
          Test 1   5 years to 8 years 11 months.
          Test 2   7 years to 11 years 11 months.
          Test 3   11 years to 18 years.

Coefficient of reliability: between ·88 and ·96 according to test used.

Order Manual, test booklet, marking template for group versions.

---

* *Reliability of a test:* This refers to a test's inbuilt capacity to yield consistent results when it is repeated. Tests with reliability coefficients of ·85 or above are very acceptable, below ·60 not very reliable measures.

READING ATTAINMENT TESTS

One of the following group tests will provide a useful measure of reading ability:

1. *The group reading test* D. Young (University of London Press)

    A group reading test which begins at a very simple picture-to-word matching level, then progresses to sentence completion items. The first section takes 4 minutes to administer, and the second section 9 minutes. Two parallel forms of the test (A and B) are available to permit class testing (half the group using form A, the remainder form B), or for retest purposes. A table in the manual provides equivalent reading ages on the Schonell, Burt, Neale, NFER *Sentence*, and Southgate test 1.

    Age range 6 years 6 months to 8 years 11 months for full range of ability. Also suitable for slow learners up to 12 years 11 months. Actual *reading ages* covered by the test 6 years to 10 years.

    Coefficient of reliability: ·94.

    Order Manual, test sheets, marking template.

2. *The graded test of reading experience, Test 12* J. C. Daniels and H. Diack (Chatto & Windus)

    This is a sentence completion test which provides a useful group screening test for upper juniors/lower secondaries. It is best to avoid giving it to *very* poor readers since they will scarcely make a start on the items: it would be better to use Young's test described above for such children. This test may be reproduced without infringing copyright.

    Age range Suitable for administration to any child whose reading age is likely to be within the range 6 years to 14 years.

    Coefficient of reliability not given.

    Order Available only in *The standard reading tests*, published by Chatto & Windus.

3. *NFER reading test AD* (Formerly *Sentence reading test 1*) A. Watts (Ginn & Co.)

    A sentence completion test, timed for 15 minutes. Norms, although compiled in 1955, were still found to be appropriate in 1965.

    Age range 7 years 6 months to 11+ years.

    Coefficient of reliability: ·94.

    Order Manual No. 41A. Test booklets 41.

4. *NFER reading test A* (Formerly *Primary reading test 1*) (Ginn & Co.)

    Sentence completion test with no time limit.

Age range 7 years to 8 years 6 months.
Coefficient of reliability not given.
Order Manual No. 229A. Test sheets 229.

5. *Southgate group reading tests* V. Southgate-Booth (University of London Press)
Test 1. A fairly simple 'word finding' test. Words are dictated by the teacher and child marks them in booklet after selecting from five possibilities. Pictures used for some items. Three parallel forms.
Age range 6 years to 7 years 6 months for normal range of ability. Also suitable for slow learners to 14 years.
Coefficient of reliability: ·95.
Order Manual for Test 1. Answer booklets for A, B, or C.
Southgate Test 2. This is a sentence completion test with two parallel forms.
Age range 7 years to 9 years 7 months, normal range ability. Also suitable for older slow learners.
Coefficient of reliability: approx. ·89.
Order Manual for Test 2. Answer booklets for form A or B.

6. *Group reading assessment* F. Spooner (University of London Press)
A group test in three sections. Part one involves 'word finding' from dictation. Part two is sentence completion. Part three is identification of homonyms (hear: here, scene: seen) in silent reading.
Age range Reading ages in the range 6+ years to 11 years 7 months. Standardised scores provided for age range 7 years 8 months to 9 years.
Coefficient of reliability: between ·91 and ·96.
Order Manual. Test booklets.

7. Schonell *Silent reading tests* F. J. Schonell (Oliver & Boyd)
Silent reading test A. (Test R3). Non-expendable test booklets. Child answers on separate slip of paper. Graded paragraph reading followed by questions to be answered. Time limit of 9 minutes.
Age range mainly useful at junior level. Reading ages given from 6 years 9 months to 12+ years, but this test has not been up-dated for some years.
Silent reading test B. (Test R4). Almost the same type of material as Test A, but at a slightly higher interest level. Non-expendable booklets. Answers written on separate sheet. Time limit of 15 minutes.

Age range suitable for top juniors and lower secondary pupils. Reading ages provided from 6 years 8 months to 13 years 6 months. Coefficient of reliability not given for either test.

Order Handbook for reading and spelling tests. Test booklets. Tests and the norms may also be consulted in the book *Diagnostic and attainment testing* published by Oliver and Boyd.

This does not exhaust the list of reading tests for group administration. Others are referred to later in the section dealing with diagnosis of reading problems. Two other group tests are worthy of mention here, however, as they are designed mainly to yield diagnostic information.

8. *The Swansea test of phonic skills* P. Williams *et al.* (Basil Blackwell Ltd.)

This is a very useful test for obtaining a rapid assessment of the phonic knowledge of a group of children. It is a 'word finding' test using nonsense syllables and words. The teacher reads out a word like *smop* which the child has to identify from five alternatives. The sixty-five items in the test sample knowledge of short vowel sounds, long vowels, consonant blends and digraphs, silent 'e' rule, etc.

Order Teacher's manual containing the 'call words'. Answer booklets.

9. *The word recognition test* C. Carver (University of London Press)

Designed to reveal overall level of word recognition ability for children with low reading ages, this test contains fifty items and the child has to find, out of a group of five or six fairly similar words a word dictated by the teacher. The child's performance on this type of material should give some indication of his phonic sight habits (does he recognise single letters from their sound values, does he recognise digraphs and blends, does he tend to reverse certain letters, etc?). The validity of such diagnostic interpretation depends very much upon the efficiency with which the test was given. Poor application in a group setting can render diagnostic interpretation useless, but individual administration is not open to the same criticism.

The norms purport to measure word recognition ages from 4 years to 8½ years. The manual *must* be carefully read for correct application and interpretation.

Order Manual. Answer sheets.

GROUP TESTS OF SPELLING ATTAINMENT

Spelling, as a topic in its own right, is dealt with later in this book.
The use of a spelling test as a screening device has not been widely
used but is advocated by Turner[14] as an aid to the identification
of juniors and seniors in need of special help.

Spelling tests have the advantages of being very easy to administer
and reasonably rapid to mark. They can also provide additional
diagnostic information about the child's ability to apply his sight
reading habits and phonic knowledge to encoding rather than
decoding words.

1. *Graded spelling tests A and B* F. J. Schonell (Oliver and Boyd)
   Graded word lists which are dictated to the children.
   Age range Suitable for children of all ages. Spelling ages given
   from 5 years to 15 years. Norms have not been revised recently.
   Order Handbook for reading and spelling tests. Graded word
   spelling test form A or form B.
   Material may also be consulted in *Diagnostic and attainment testing*.

2. *Graded spelling test, Test 11* J. C. Daniels and H. Diack (Chatto &
   Windus Ltd.)
   A graded list of 40 words to be dictated by the teacher. The
   words are sub-divided into four sets according to difficulty.
   Age range Suitable for any child. Spelling ages given from 5 years
   to 12+ years.
   Order Only available in the book *The standard reading tests*.

3. *Graded dictation tests* F. J. Schonell and G. Sleight (Macmillan Co.
   Ltd.)
   Six paragraphs, carefully graded in difficulty, which are dictated
   to the group. Errors in the test are converted to a positive score,
   which in turn yields an approximate spelling age in the range
   7 years to 13 years. Results are very useful for diagnostic purposes.
   The graded dictation tests are presented in the book *Essentials
   in teaching and testing spelling*, published by Macmillan.

GROUP TESTS OF NUMBER AND MATHEMATICS

These are dealt with in the main section on assessment of number
difficulties (Chapter 6).

GROUP TESTS OF NON-VERBAL MENTAL ABILITY

If teachers require a measure of non-verbal mental ability with which
to compare verbal ability the following tests are suitable:

1. NFER *Picture test A* (Formerly *Picture test 1*) J. Stuart (Ginn & Co.)
   Three sub-tests with a total of 60 items. Time limit approximately
   40 minutes.
   Age range 7 years to 8 years.
   Coefficient of reliability: ·92.
   Order Manual 42A. Test 42.
2. NFER *Non-verbal test BD* (Formerly *Non-verbal test 5*) D. Pidgeon
   (Ginn & Co.)
   Four sub-tests with a total of 100 items. Time 40 minutes.
   Age range 8 years to 11 years.
   Coefficient of reliability: ·94.
   Order Manual 28A. Test 28.
3. NFER *Non-verbal test DH* (Formerly *Non-verbal test 3*) B. Calvert
   (Ginn & Co.)
   Two main sub-sections with a total of 96 items. Time 50 minutes.
   Shorter version also possible using same booklets. Time 35 minutes.
   Test booklets are non-expendable. Answer sheets need to be
   ordered.
   Age range 10 years to 15 years.
   Coefficient of reliability: ·95.
   Order Manual and Template 15A. Test booklets 15. Answer sheets
   15B.
4. *Moray House picture intelligence tests 1 and* 2 G. Thomson and
   M. Mellone (University of London Press)
   Nine sub-tests. 100 items.
   Age range 6 years 6 months to 8 years.
   Coefficient of reliability: ·95.
   Order Manual MH (PIC) 1. Test sheets; Manual MH (PIC) 2.
   Test sheets.
5. *Deeside picture test for seven year-olds* W. Emmett (Harrap Co. Ltd.)
   Seven sub-tests with a total of 100 items. Total time required
   for administration is approximately one hour (actual working
   time 25 minutes). Picture material is used throughout, but the
   test involves a great deal of listening comprehension.
   Age range 6 years 6 months to 8 years 6 months.
   Coefficient of reliability: ·96.
   Order Manual. Test booklets.

This list does not exhaust the range of tests available for classroom
use. Teachers who require tests to assess verbal reasoning in pupils
who are *not* backward in reading, or who require tests to assess

progress in English or Mathematics at secondary school level, should consult the current catalogue from Ginn & Co., Test Services, the books by Jackson[4] or Labon[6] or the ACER catalogue.

Diagnostic testing

The difference between attainment and diagnostic testing is stated clearly by Schonell:[12] 'The fundamental principle in the interpretation of diagnostic tests is that the *qualitative* examination of the testee's work is much more important than any quantitative estimates of it' (p. 30).

The purposes of diagnostic testing may be summarised as:

(i) to discover within a particular skill area precisely what a child *can* do already and has mastered;

(ii) to locate the point of failure or misunderstanding and isolate the specific difficulties;

(iii) to gain information which will indicate the next step required in the teaching programme;

(iv) to identify any deficiencies in underlying skills or processes which may need highly specific remediation or, in some cases, may indicate a need to select a teaching method which will bypass the weakness.

These points will be dealt with more fully in the later sections of the book.

Diagnostic testing, if carefully carried out, yields far more valuable information with implications for teaching than does attainment testing alone. Diagnostic *testing* should lead to diagnostic *teaching*—a term which implies that a particular approach to a child's problems has been adopted after careful consideration of his strengths and weaknesses, and has, over a period of time, been modified in ways which appear to result in optimum progress by the child. To be of any real value, diagnostic testing must be carried out with the individual child, in a quiet situation and relaxed atmosphere, by a teacher who has the child's full co-operation and confidence. Just as the success of remedial teaching is very much dependent upon the relationship established between teacher and child so, too, the validity of diagnostic procedures is similarly affected.

In-depth diagnostic assessment, such as that recommended in the following sections, should be carried out over a period of days or weeks, working only for as long as the child is able to do his best.

Schonell[12] warned that diagnostic testing should never be continued to the point of fatigue, an important fact often overlooked by the over-zealous.

Suggestions for further study

(a) Examine at least one test from each of the sections on verbal ability, non-verbal ability and reading. Try to administer one of of the group tests to a class of primary or secondary children. What are the snags and difficulties encountered on the first occasion?

(b) The term *reliability* has been explained in this section. Find out the meaning of the term *validity* as applied to a test. Also try to discover what is meant by the term *error of measurement*. Why is it important to have some idea of the error of measurement associated with a particular test you have given?

(c) The whole vexed question of the nature of intelligence remains unresolved. A teacher's own views concerning the nature of intelligence can significantly influence his outlook in teaching children with learning difficulties: he is either optimistic or pessimistic in his approach.

Vernon[16] has said, '... intelligence is not a single, unitary entity: it comprises a host of overlapping functions which doubtless develop at different rates at different times' (p. 103).

The following statements indicate the extremes of conflicting views on the nature of intelligence testing:

(i) 'A test of general intelligence or mental ability is designed to estimate innate mental ability rather than acquired knowledge.'[12]

(ii) 'It is always the child's level of *acquired* abilities that is available for testing, not the child's capacity or his mental potentiality ... tests measure the acquisition of the abilities rather than the capacity.'[13]

Reappraise your own views concerning the nature of intelligence. The following books may prove useful:

BUTCHER, H. J. (1968) *Human intelligence: its nature and assessment,* London, Methuen.

BUTCHER, H. J. and LOMAX, D. (eds.) (1972) *Readings in human intelligence,* London, Methuen.

DOCKRELL, W. (ed.) (1970) *On intelligence. The Toronto symposium*, London, Methuen.

VERNON, P. E. (1969) *Intelligence and cultural environment*, London, Methuen.

WISEMAN, S. (1967) *Intelligence and ability*, Harmondsworth, Penguin Books.

References

1. CROWTHER, G. R. (1971) Educational screening: a pilot report, *Remedial Education*, **6**, No. 2, 37–9.
2. GULLIFORD, R. (1971) *Special educational needs*, London, Routledge & Kegan Paul.
3. HUNT, J. Mc. V. (1961) *Intelligence and experience*, New York, Ronald Press.
4. JACKSON, S. (1968) *A Teacher's guide to tests*, London, Longman.
5. KIRK, S. A. (1973) 'The education of intelligence,' *The slow learning child*, **20**, 67–83.
6. LABON, D. (1972) *Assessment of intelligence*, Chichester, West Sussex Psychological Service Publication.
7. LYTTON, H. (1968) 'Selection for remedial education,' *Remedial Education*, **3**, No. 2, 66–9.
8. O'KELLY, E. (1970) 'A method for detecting slow learning juniors,' *Educational Research*, **12**, 135–9.
9. PHILLIPS, C. J. (1968) 'The future of remedial education services,' *Remedial Education*, **3**, No. 2, 70–3.
10. RUSSELL, J. (1970) 'Reading surveys,' *Reading* (UKRA), **4**, 13–8.
11. SAVAGE, R. D. (1968) *Psychometric assessment of the individual child*, Harmondsworth, Penguin Books.
12. SCHONELL, F. J. and SCHONELL, F. E. (1960) *Diagnostic and attainment testing* (4th Ed.), Edinburgh, Oliver and Boyd.
13. STOTT, L. and BALL, R. (1965) *Infant and pre-school mental tests: review and evaluation* (*Soc. for Research in Child Development, Monograph 30*, No. 3), Chicago, University of Chicago Press.
14. TURNER, B. (1971) 'The use of a spelling test as a screening device,' *Remedial Education*, **6**, No. 1, 31–3.
15. VERNON, P. (1960) 'The classification of abilities,' *Educational Research*, **2**, *184–93*.
16. VERNON, P. (1960) *Intelligence and attainment testing*, London, University of London Press.
17. WILLIAMS, A. (1970) *Basic subjects for slow learners*, London, Methuen.
18. YOUNG, D. (1968) *Manual* for *The group reading test*, London, University of London Press.
19. *Tests for guidance and assessment*, published for NFER. Free from Ginn & Co. Test Services. Elsinore House, Buckingham Street, Aylesbury, Bucks.

Recommended reading

JACKSON, S. (1971) *A teacher's guide to tests and testing* (2nd Ed.), London, Longman.
SCHOFIELD, H. (1972) *Assessment and testing: an introduction*, London, Allen and Unwin.
WOMER, F. B. (1968) *Basic concepts in testing*, Boston, Hougton Mifflin.

More advanced

KAHN, T. and GRIFFEN, M. (1960) *Psychological techniques in diagnosis and evaluation*, London, Pergamon Press.
MITTLER, O. (ed.) (1970) *The psychological assessment of mental and physical handicaps*, London, Methuen.
SAVAGE, D. (1968) *The psychometric assessment of the individual child*, Harmondsworth, Penguin Books.
STANLEY, J. C. and HOPKINS, K. D. (1972) *Educational and psychological measurement and evaluation*, Englewood-Cliffs, New Jersey, Prentice-Hall.

3. The assessment of oral language

There is a gulf between those who have, and the many who have not, sufficient command of words to be able to listen and discuss rationally; to express ideas and feelings clearly; and even to have any ideas at all. We simply do not know how many people are frustrated in their lives by inability ever to express themselves adequately; or how many never develop intellectually because they lack the words with which to think and to reason.[12]

The child's ability to process language in school is perhaps the most important factor in his intellectual and educational growth. The improvement of language skills, therefore, ranks high as a goal of adaptive, compensatory and remedial education.

Thought processes are heavily dependent upon language competence. Language is essential for concept acquisition beyond a very elementary level. [3][19] It is for that reason that the importance of verbal intelligence was stressed in the previous chapter.

Most teachers are aware that certain children are obviously retarded in their language development, or have difficulty in communicating efficiently; yet very little is done to alleviate the problem. A teacher will attempt to do something positive to help the child who is backward in reading, or who is experiencing difficulties in mathematics; but there is a tendency to accept oral language deficiencies as 'inevitable'. There seems to be an assumption that if we place a child in an environment where language is used freely some of this is bound to rub off on the disadvantaged slow learner. System, structure and clearly defined goals are completely lacking; yet these are considered vital in remediation programmes for other skill areas. Even in the infant school a child may develop a 'learned inattention' to the teacher's voice. The teacher unintentionally employs a language structure which is more complex than the child has experienced before, and uses some words which the child does not understand. Very soon the child begins to expect not to know what teachers are talking about, so henceforth never listens. A poor level of listening skill is characteristic of many slow learners, ... in some cases it is school-induced!

It is essential that something positive is done to improve the language skill of children with marked deficiencies in this area. Planned intervention should follow assessment of the child's present functional level and diagnosis of the particular difficulties.

The evaluation of oral language performance needs to be made along several lines. For the average teacher in school, the detailed assessment made possible by such diagnostic instruments as *The Illinois test of psycholinguistic abilities*[8] or *The Reynell developmental language scales*[14] is out of the question, but a systematic appraisal can be attempted following some of the suggestions given below. The results should give some indication of an individual child's specific needs and, therefore, what should be covered in a language improvement programme.

Communication through the medium of spoken language has two broad aspects, which Wilkinson[19] refers to as *Reception* and *Production*, and in the realm of 'oracy' are reflected in *Listening* and *Speaking*. Osgood[13] uses the terms *Decoding* and *Encoding*. Reynell[14] considers that since the receptive and expressive aspects of language are different as processes they are worthy of separate appraisal.

The evaluation of receptive aspects

(i) *Assessing receptive vocabulary*

This can very suitably be accomplished through the use of the *English picture vocabulary tests* (*EPVT*). These tests cover the age range 3 years to 18 years and do not require a spoken response from the child. Although there is a reasonably high correlation between performance on the *EPVT* and tests of verbal intelligence, the results from *EPVT* should not be regarded as indicating an intelligence level. The score is more usefully viewed as showing the child to be above average, average, or below average in his language experience. A low score on *EPVT* implies the need (a) for the teacher to make allowance for the child's probable difficulties in understanding what is said to him unless conveyed in simple terms, and (b) to aim deliberately at increasing the child's receptive vocabulary. (Teaching points are made more explicit in the section on language remediation later in this book.)

A more informal assessment of a child's receptive vocabulary can be made using picture material. Suitable colourful and interesting pictures can be made the focal point for sampling a child's understanding of nouns, adjectives, and adverbs. The child is asked, for instance, 'Show me something *tall* in the picture'. 'Show me something which could move *very fast*'. 'Point to the *smallest* tree'. The use of 'show me' or 'point to' rather than 'tell me' is deliberate: here we are concerned whether the child understands the word and the instruction, not to impose the added difficulty of having to express a verbal reply.

Toys or common objects may be used to determine a child's grasp of prepositions ('put this *behind* the chair'; 'put this *between* the cars').

It is sometimes necessary to assess a child's receptive vocabulary connected with a particular subject. This is very important in mathematics, where a teacher may use very unfamiliar words in an attempt to teach or explain some relationship (for example, 'amount'; 'altogether'; 'curve'; 'shape'). We should not always assume that these are fully understood.

Sometimes a failure to understand the two words 'same' and 'different' can invalidate a child's responses to some tests (for instance, in replying to a personality and attitude questionnaire; to performing on an auditory discrimination test; to responding to some conservation of number tests).

Although there are no norms against which to judge a child's performance if the teacher has devised her own receptive language assessment, even a subjective evaluation will reveal as much about a child's present limitations and needs as will a more clinical test. The Auditory Reception Test in *The Illinois test of psycholinguistic abilities*[8] assesses the child's receptive language by posing such questions as, 'Do chairs eat?'; 'Do pavements sprinkle?'; 'Do sausages frown?' The child replies 'yes' or 'no'. Used in or out of the context of the complete *ITPA* this sub-test does not, in itself, yield much diagnostic information apart from the fact that the child's vocabulary is, perhaps, limited.

(ii) *Test of the understanding of the spoken word*

This very useful little test was devised by Coral Richards in 1964 for use with children aged three to six years. It has also been found useful with junior children who have language difficulties and with educationally subnormal children in the primary range.

The kit comprises four rooms of dolls' house furniture and equipment, which allows the tester to sample the child's vocabulary (including prepositions); even more important, it enables the teacher to detect the point at which the child begins to fail to understand spoken instructions. The test instructions gradually become more complex and it is easy to identify the maximum length and complexity of instruction which the child can retain and carry out. This insight into the child's receptive problems has a direct bearing on how the teacher will need to shape her own language to communicate successfully with that child.

Details of the source of this useful test are presented in Appendix 4.

(iii) *Short-term auditory memory*

Menyuk[10] and Masland and Case[9] have indicated that short-term memory span may significantly influence early language development, while Graham[6] suggests that short-term memory deficiency may well be the main culprit in disrupting cognitive functioning. His research has indicated that limitations of immediate memory may influence a child's ability to process language which he hears or which he needs in order to express himself. Short-term memory problems are also associated with some difficulties in reading—a point to be developed in the next chapter.

One routine assessment which should be made of any child with possible language problems is his short-term retention span for meaningful material. Few sentence repetition tests exist for the teacher to use; those that do are either designed for the very young child only, or were prepared for research work concerned with children's ability to use different grammatical and syntactical forms.

A simple sentence repetition test is included in the teacher's manual *Getting ready for reading* by E. H. Grassam (Ginn and Co). It is suggested that children should be able to repeat at least five out of ten simple six-word sentences correctly: for example, 'What shall we have for dinner?'; 'We go to bed at night'; 'We get up in the morning'. Children who cannot do this may not be ready for certain demands which reading places upon them, and may be exhibiting one symptom of hearing problems and/or poor memory span.

By the age of five most children should be able to remember and carry out a triple order: for instance, 'Do you see this key? Go and put it on the table. Then shut the door. And after that, bring me the book that is on the chair near the door. Do you understand? First put the key on the table; then shut the door; then bring me the book'.[1]

Some child-development experts have attempted to summarise the increasing short-term memory span of the growing child by indicating the number of syllables he is capable of repeating at various age levels. They have failed to agree on figures because the length of a sentence in terms of syllables is less important than its actual grammatical structure, and even less important than the degree of meaning which the sentence does, or does not, convey to the child. To say, therefore, that at the age of five years a child can repeat 10 syllables, at six years he can repeat 16 syllables, and at fourteen years 26 syllables is inaccurate and misleading. It is more useful to discover a particular child's limits by working on simple sentences and phrases, and to use a sentence repetition test as a screening device to identify those who have great difficulty in repeating simple statements.

The test below is a modified form of one used in a research project with lower juniors,[18] and has a reliability coefficient of ·81. Children who begin to fail at or before sentence 5 may require special help with receptive aspects of language (see later sections); and the teacher must almost certainly take such deficiency into account when explaining something to the child, or when giving instructions.

Sentence repetition test

1. Mother.
2. My knife and fork.
3. I am cold and hungry.
4. Here is the cloth; my hands are clean.
5. His name is Tim; he's such a naughty dog.
6. It is raining outside and Tom is working hard.
7. We are having a funny game: I like it very much.
8. We are going for a walk; will you give me that nice new jacket.
9. Linda has just torn her frock so I have given it to that poor neighbour.
10. We should never be cruel to animals because a kind person is much nicer.

Each sentence is said *once* only to the child who must then repeat it in exactly the same form. The word 'listen' is said before each sentence to catch the child's attention.

The evaluation of expressive aspects

(i) *Vocabulary*

If expressive aspects of language are to be evaluated it is usually better to use a vocabulary test which requires the child to give the definition of a word orally rather than point to a picture to illustrate it.

Suitable tests of this type are:

The Crichton vocabulary scale This oral definitions test devised by J. C. Raven (Lewis and Co.) covers the age range four and a half to eleven years.

The Mill Hill vocabulary scale This test can be administered as an oral definition assessment or, for those who can read and write, a written form with separate norms can be applied. The oral form covers the age range 4½ to 14 years. The written form covers the age range 11½ to 25 years. *The Mill Hill scale* was also devised by J. C. Raven.

The Holborn vocabulary test for young children This test devised by A. F. Watts (Harrap) covers the age range 3½ to 8½ years. It contains 100 items and can be quite time-consuming to apply.

(ii) *Articulation*

The assessment of articulation is usually left to the speech therapist or clinician. However, it can be very helpful for a remedial teacher to have some idea of the basic speech sounds which a particular child cannot yet produce correctly; but it should be stressed that if a child's speech is obviously defective it is essential that the advice of a specialist be obtained. Caution needs to be exercised in judging when it is appropriate to leave speech correction in the hands of a remedial teacher; but it is equally true that many children with minor speech problems receive no help at all when, in fact, the teacher could be of great help to them. For this reason remedial teachers may usefully add the following test to their repertoire, and may find the books listed under *Speech* in Appendix 5 helpful.

The Goldman-Fristoe *Test of articulation* (Educational Evaluation Enterprises) is simple to apply and consists of colourful picture material for testing 35 basic speech sounds sampled in the initial, medial, and final positions. The child merely replies to simple questions about the pictures, and colour-coding on the teacher's recording sheet permits easy identification of the particular sound sampled within the words of the answer.

A child's articulation skill needs to be viewed against (a) his own chronological age, and (b) the quality of his auditory discrimination (see page 48).

(iii) *The evaluation of a language sample*

One technique which has been used over the years for research purposes is the quantitative and qualitative evaluation of a sample of the child's spoken language.

As yet there is no *standard* method for obtaining a language sample. Toys, pictures, films, informal conversation and the retelling of a familiar story have all been used by investigators to elicit a sample of language, but this procedure is far less accurate than, for example, the administration of a standardised reading test. A child's perform-ance is known to be influenced by such variables as the type of material used to elicit the speech, the age, sex and social-class of the examiner, the amount of praise and encouragement given, and the physical situation in which the interview took place.[2][5] Nevertheless, provided that the teacher realises the imperfections in the method, and goes for a qualitative rather than a quantitative evaluation the technique is well worth applying with any child whose expressive use of language seems very restricted.

The normal procedure is to obtain a sample of at least 60 utterances made by the child in, for example, describing a set of pictures and then talking about his interests at home, or in school, or on television. The responses are recorded on tape for later transcription. In transcribing the material the first 10 utterances produced while the child is adjusting to the situation are discarded leaving a corpus of exactly 50 responses for analysis.[7][17] Fifty responses are considered just about adequate for a reliable sample.[4]

A response, or 'utterance', is identified by a natural break in the child's verbalisation; a 'per-breath' statement marked off from the next by a pause. The two short samples below indicate that an utterance is not necessarily equivalent to a grammatically correct and complete sentence. The presence of the word 'and' doesn't necessarily indicate that it is functioning as a conjunction: frequently it is used as an 'opener', just as the words 'Well' or 'Oh' may serve to begin a remark.

EXAMPLES:

(a) **Terry**

Chronological Age 7 years 8 months.

From large family.   Verbal IQ 84.   Non-verbal IQ 98.

Working class.   A non-reader.

Picture 5

'They all goin' shoppin / and they buyin' things. / There's church. / And there apples . . . er . . . an' presents. / And it called Ashton. / Two buses. /'

Television interests [Spiderman]

'He gets a thingy and . . . er. / He gets one of them . . . things. / He fly. / Er . . . yes, news. / Er . . . ship blewed up. / It's about army . . . er. / Tom and Jerry . . . er . . . they. / Can't remember now. / The . . . the lady dived in t'water, like. / Er . . . did a som . . . er . . . a . . . oh . . . er . . . somersort. / They get cards and er. / They tell 'tories. / Er . . . make . . . er . . . moggles.'

(b) **Helen**

Chronological Age 7 years 8 months.

Only two girls in family.   Verbal IQ 129. Non-verbal IQ 98.

Social Class II. Reading Age 9·2 years.

Picture 5

'Um . . . there's a statue and the names of all people what died. / And there's a man sellin', don't know, oranges or something. / And um . . . there's something, a building called Castle. / And there's a new kind of . . . er . . . a cafe, I think it is. / And there's a bus near it. / There's a stall selling f . . . er fly . . . flyspray. / And there's a lady wearing a fur coat somewhere there, look. /'

Television interests [Blue Peter]

'They show you things to make and things to go to. / Um . . . they got Blue Peter II out to a place and they did it in twelve minutes, it took. / The other person had got in the yacht already and tried to get home. / [On the Buses] Well, one day they bashed into a pair of traffic lights. / And . . . um . . . they tried not to show the dint to Blakey. /'

In neither case has the full sample of 50 utterances been reproduced.

A quantitative analysis of a sample usually involves the counting of the total number of words used in producing the 50 utterances (excluding the 'ums', 'ers', etc). Contractions (there's = there is) count as two words. The total number of words is usually divided by 50 to give the *mean length of utterance*. Other useful measures which reflect maturity or lack of it are (a) finding the mean length of the child's *five longest utterances*, and (b) counting the number of *one-word utterances* used. Templin[16] provides norms for these measures indicating, for example, that an average child whose chronological age is three years uses roughly four words per utterance compared with roughly seven and a half words per utterance at eight years. The three-year-old uses roughly eight words in his longest utterances while the eight-year-old uses 14 words. The three-year-old uses roughly six one-word responses, which, by the age of eight years, have been reduced to less than one.

Diagnostically, it is more valuable to examine the *quality* of the child's spoken language. Does he use adjectives, adverbs, prepositions? Has he grasped the correct form of plurals? Does he use the appropriate verb tense to suit the statement? Answers to questions like these will have a bearing on the language remediation programme which may be required for the child. (See chapter 9.)

Before analysing a language sample teachers are advised to read the book by Templin,[16] or that by Johnson *et al.*[7] For a more sophisticated evaluation of language, required perhaps for clinical therapy purposes, the reader is referred to the *Length-complexity scoring system* (Shriner & Sherman[15] and Miner[11]).

(iv)　*Familiarity with language patterns*

The child who is constantly exposed to stimulating language experience and to correct language models *should* become so familiar with common language patterns that these become 'habit' responses. He should be able to predict the next word in a flow of speech and mentally be capable of 'closing' an unfinished statement or phrase:[19] for example, 'Once upon a ...'; 'He rang the ...'; 'She put the hat on her ....' Osgood's theoretical model of communication processes identified a level which he termed *integrational level*—the one at which a person makes use of the redundancies of frequently used language patterns.[13] Kirk & McCarthy describe this as the *automatic level* of performance—the processing of language without the need for planning and careful thought. They sample it in the *ITPA* in the Grammatic Closure sub-test. The child is asked to complete unfinished statements: for example, 'Here is a child. Here are three ... [children]'; 'This boy had two bananas. He gave one away, but he kept one for ... [himself].' The items are supported by picture material.[8] A teacher can devise similar discussion/story situations for testing a child's ability to complete familiar sentence structures.

(v)   *Tests of Proficiency in English 1973* (Ginn, for NFER)

Designed to test proficiency in listening, speaking, reading and writing in children from seven to eleven years. Also suitable for use with immigrant children.

Suggestions for further study

(a) Obtain a language sample (50 utterances) from one of your least able children. What does it reveal about his/her functional level in expressive language?

How might you structure the situation to sample in particular the child's fund of adjectives and adverbs?

(b) List some of the words which are peculiar to a particular subject area (mathematics, science, cookery, P.E., etc). Select words which a teacher might easily use in talking with a class of children in the age range nine to twelve years. Use the material as a list to check whether one of your less able children can define these words.

References

1. BURT, C. (1962) *Mental and scholastic tests* (4th Ed.), London, Staples Press.
2. COWAN, P., WEBER, J., HODDINOTT, B. and KLEIN, J. (1967) 'Mean length of spoken response as a function of stimulus, experimenter, and subject,' *Child Development*, **38**, 191–203.
3. CREBER, J. W. (1972) *Lost for words*, Harmondsworth, Penguin Books.
4. DARLEY, F. and MOLL, K. (1960) 'Reliability of language measures and size of sample,' *Journal of Speech and Hearing Research*, **3**, 166–73.
5. DICKIE, J. and BAGUR, J. (1972) 'Considerations for the study of language in young low-income minority group children,' *Merrill-Palmer Qtly.* **18**, 25–38.
6. GRAHAM, N. C. (1968) 'A psycholinguistic approach to language deficiency' in *The child and the outside world*, Association for Special Education.
7. JOHNSON, W., DARLEY, F. and SPRIESTERSBACH, D. (1963) *Diagnostic methods in speech pathology*, New York, Harper and Row.

8. KIRK, S. and McCARTHY, J. (1968) *The Illinois test of psycholinguistic abilities,* Urbana, University of Illinois Press.
9. MASLAND, M. and CASE, L. (1968) 'Limitation of auditory memory as a factor in delayed language development,' *Brit. Journal Disorders of Communication,* **3,** 139–12.
10. MENYUK, P. (1969) *Sentences children use,* Cambridge, Mass., M.I.T. Press.
11. MINER, L. E. (1969) 'Scoring procedure for the length-complexity index,' *Journal of Communication Disorders,* **2,** 224–40.
12. Ministry of Education (1963) *Half our future: the Newsom Report,* London, H.M.S.O.
13. OSGOOD, C. E. (1957) 'A behaviouristic analysis of perception and language' in *Contemporary approaches to cognition,* 75–118, Cambridge, Mass., Harvard University Press.
14. REYNELL, J. (1969) *The Reynell developmental language scales,* Slough, NFER.
15. SHRINER, T. and SHERMAN, D. (1967) 'An equation for assessing language development, '*Journal of Speech and Hearing Research,* **10,** 41–8.
16. TEMPLIN, M. (1957) *Certain language skills in children,* Minneapolis, University of Minnesota Press.
17. TYACK, D. (1973) 'The uses of language samples in a clinical setting,' *Journal of Learning Disabilities,* **6,** 213–6.
18. WESTWOOD, P. (1973) *Predicting expressive and receptive language performance from measures of psycholinguistic abilities,* unpublished Master's Degree Thesis, University of Manchester.
19. WILKINSON, A. (1971) *The foundations of language,* London, Oxford University Press.

Recommended reading

BRITTON, J. (1970) *Language and learning,* Harmondsworth, Penguin Books.
CREBER, J. (1972) *Lost for words,* Harmondsworth, Penguin Books.
HERRIOT, P. (1971) *Language and teaching,* London, Methuen.
LAWTON, D. (1968) *Social class, language and education,* London, Routledge.
TOUGH, J. (1976) *Listening to Children Talking,* London, Ward Lock.

More advanced

BERRY, M. F. (1969) *Language disorders of children,* New York, Appleton-Century-Crofts.
CAZDEN, C. (1972) *Child language and education,* London and New York, Holt, Rinehart, and Winston.

4. The in-depth assessment of reading skills

In this chapter several different tests are named as suitable for various aspects of assessment: it is not necessary for a remedial teacher to obtain all the tests described. They merely reflect what is available for use and may already be in stock in the school or the local resources centre.

Although an experienced remedial teacher can usually obtain most of the important information concerning a child's present reading level, phonic knowledge, word-attack skills and comprehension within the period of twenty to thirty minutes of testing, in-depth evaluation takes longer. It also needs to be spread over several sessions with the child. The diagnostic programme below obviously should not be attempted at one sitting if it is to yield valid and reliable information. Carefully applied, the programme will reveal the child's needs and will guide the planning of an individualised reading programme.

Diagnostic testing follows a logical sequence of posing the right questions in the right order. The basic sequence will first be summarised, then each stage dealt with in detail.

Individual diagnostic programme

PHASE I

The first three questions will be posed for any child presented for diagnostic assessment in reading.

*Q*1 What is the child's present functional level in reading?

This will be indicated roughly from the results of a group screening test; but at this stage an individual test should be selected from those listed on page 41. It is worth recording the result both as a reading age and as a reading quotient

$$\left(\frac{\text{R.A.}}{\text{C.A.}} \times 100 = \text{R.Q.} \right).$$

39

A reading quotient gives a better indication of progress made when the child is retested after a lengthy remedial course.

Q2 How does the child's reading age compare with his general expressive and receptive language ability?

As a very minimum, a vocabulary test should be applied. If time permits and if oral language appears a major problem with this child, evaluate along the lines suggested in chapter 3 of this book (pp. 29–37).

Q3 How does the child's reading performance compare with his verbal mental ability?

One of Young's *Oral verbal intelligence tests* from University of London Press will provide a useful measure here. These were referred to on page 18.

Phase ii

Certain questions from the following set will be asked according to the child's present level in reading revealed by Q1 above.

Q4 What can the child do already in terms of whole-word recognition?

Q5 What can he do already in terms of phonic analysis and synthesis of words?

Q6 If the child is a non-reader has he developed adequate speech, visual perceptual and auditory perceptual skills to begin reading?

Q7 If the child has made a slight start in reading is he ready for a positive and systematic introduction to phonics and word-building?

Q8 If the child is reasonably proficient but has reached a sticking point or plateau, what kind of mistakes is he making within his reading performance?

Q9 What is his level of comprehension?

It is pointless to ask any of the above questions from Phase i and Phase ii unless the answers influence the future teaching programme for that child.

PHASE I SUITABLE TESTS FOR ASSESSING FUNCTIONAL READING LEVEL

Where possible it is best to select from the following list a test which will permit the child's reading age to fall within the test's middle ranges, as all tests tend to be unreliable at the upper and lower extremes of their scale. Obviously, it is not always possible to meet this requirement if the child is of very low reading attainment.

Remember that it is always useful to note the errors which a child makes in performing on the individual test. These may show whether or not he has developed some phonic knowledge and word attack skills. Always encourage the child to try a word rather than refuse.

Children soon memorise parts of tests through constantly hearing others read them aloud, and for this reason care should be taken to avoid the frequent use of reading tests performed aloud in the classroom setting.

(i) *Standard reading test 1* Daniels and Diack (1958, Chatto & Windus)

Sentence material to be read aloud. This test is most useful if the child's reading age is likely to be between Nil and eight years, although the test book provides reading ages to nine years.

The test book contains follow-up diagnostic tests which will be dealt with in later sections below.

(ii) *Analysis of reading ability* M. Neale (1966, Macmillan)

Covers reading ages from 6 to 13 years

The test uses meaningful prose passages to be read aloud. The single test can yield separate measures of reading accuracy, comprehension and speed of reading. Three parallel forms of the test are available and a recording sheet enables the teacher to carry out an analysis of the errors made by the child. The test booklet also includes three short diagnostic tests covering knowledge of letter sounds, auditory discrimination through simple spelling, blending and recognition of syllables. This test becomes a very useful instrument at the point where the *Standard test 1* ceases to be of much value, but the interest levels of the early passages on each form are aimed at lower junior level.

(iii) *Graded word reading test R1*, F. J. Schonell (1950, Oliver & Boyd)

A graded list of isolated words to be read aloud. Child cannot make use of context to 'guess'. A reliable test which takes little time to administer. If the word list is used the recent (1970) norms beginning at the more realistic reading age of six, not five years as previously, should be consulted.

(iv) *The Burt rearranged word reading test*, Burt-Vernon (1969, U.L.P)

Also a graded list of isolated words, but beginning at an easier level than Test R1 above. New norms for this test (1972) are given in Appendix 2.

The ACER word identification test is a suitable substitute for (iii) and (iv) above (ACER, 1972).

(v) *Marino graded word reading scale*, S. V. O'Suilleabhain (1970, Longman, Brown & Nolan, Dublin)

For assessing reading levels of young people in Ireland. Reading ages from five to nineteen years. A very informative manual is provided.

(vi) *The Holborn sentence scale*, A. Watts (1948, Harrap)

Sentence reading material to be read aloud. For reading ages 5 years 9 months to 13 years. The norms are in need of revision, but the test is still widely used in schools.

(vii) *The Edinburgh reading tests*, Godfrey Thomson Unit (1973, U.L.P. and Moray House College of Education, Edinburgh)

These tests are available for group or individual administration. Stage 1 covers ages 7 to 9 years. Stage 2 covers $8\frac{1}{2}$–$10\frac{1}{2}$ years. Stage 3 covers 10 to $12\frac{1}{2}$ years. Stage 4 for ages above 12 years.

The battery makes use of a very valuable form of *profiling* to highlight a child's relative strengths and weaknesses across a range of reading skills. It is to be hoped that these tests will become widely used in the future. Norms are available for England, Scotland, and Wales.

RESULTS FROM PHASE I

The test given may yield one of the following results:

(a) The child is not yet reading at all, and may indeed be at a pre-reading level (STAGE 0);* (b) The child has made a slight start in reading and knows a few words by sight (STAGE 1);* (c) The child is progressing at an elementary level using mainly a whole-word recognition (look and say) approach (STAGE 2);* (d) The child reveals some basic decoding skills (phonic knowledge) but word building skills not fully developed (STAGE 3);* (e) The child is a reasonable reader but has specific gaps in his knowledge and may have reached a temporary plateau (STAGE 4);* (f) The child who is ten years or older is reading at a standard normal for his/her age and general verbal ability (STAGE 5).*

It is extremely difficult (if not impossible) to equate precise reading ages with each of the above STAGES of reading development, and it has been pointed out already that different reading tests yield different reading ages. It is now generally accepted that reading ages much below six years are virtually meaningless,[1][11][12] although some reading tests purport to measure ages down to four years. The other important point is that the STAGE which a child has reached really depends upon the extent of his development of certain component skills (phonic skill, use of context, comprehension, etc). This information is far more important than that provided by a global reading age of, say, 7·3 years which reveals nothing about the child's underlying skills. For these reasons the ages presented in fig. 1 (page 44) and in the following sections should be taken as a very rough guide. Assessments suggested for one STAGE may well be very appropriate for a child whose reading age places him just outside that STAGE; there is considerable overlap.

The relative importance of a child's present stage of reading development should be viewed against his present chronological age and general language and intellectual ability. This need to consider verbal ability and age alongside reading performance does not mean that these set a permanent limit on his chances of improvement, or indeed predict the *rate* of progress, but they can indicate whether in a particular child's case, a language enrichment and extension programme will be needed just as much as a remedial reading programme.

---

* These STAGES should not be confused with the term 'reading standard' used by Daniels and Diack.[2] These STAGES correspond with similar 'levels of instruction' later in the book.

Fig. 1

Summary of in-depth evaluation of reading performance

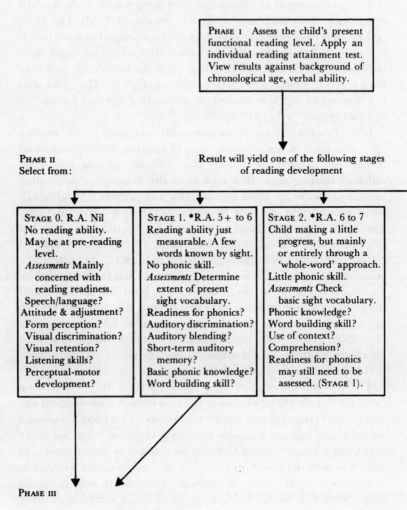

PHASE I Assess the child's present functional reading level. Apply an individual reading attainment test. View results against background of chronological age, verbal ability.

PHASE II
Select from:

Result will yield one of the following stages of reading development

STAGE 0. R.A. Nil
No reading ability.
May be at pre-reading level.
Assessments Mainly concerned with reading readiness.
Speech/language?
Attitude & adjustment?
Form perception?
Visual discrimination?
Visual retention?
Listening skills?
Perceptual-motor development?

STAGE 1. *R.A. 5+ to 6
Reading ability just measurable. A few words known by sight.
No phonic skill.
Assessments Determine extent of present sight vocabulary.
Readiness for phonics?
Auditory discrimination?
Auditory blending?
Short-term auditory memory?
Basic phonic knowledge?
Word building skill?

STAGE 2. *R.A. 6 to 7
Child making a little progress, but mainly or entirely through a 'whole-word' approach.
Little phonic skill.
Assessments Check basic sight vocabulary.
Phonic knowledge?
Word building skill?
Use of context?
Comprehension?
Readiness for phonics may still need to be assessed. (STAGE 1).

PHASE III

For just a few individuals deeper assessment of auditory and visual perception.

(* Reading ages must be regarded as very approximate.)

STAGE 3. *R.A. 7 to 8	STAGE 4. *R.A. 8 to 9+	STAGE 5. *R.A. 9½ years and above.

Some evidence of phonic skills but not fully developed.
Assessment Check full extent of sight vocabulary.
Check phonic knowledge in detail.
  Common single-letter sounds?
  Consonant digraphs & blends as sight habits?
  Vowel digraphs and blends?
Word-building skill?
Spelling ability?
Comprehension?
	Child is a reasonable reader but has reached a plateau or has significant weaknesses.
	Assessment Analysis of reading errors.
	Higher level word attack skills?
	Spelling ability?
	Comprehension?
	Use of context?
		Reading age may be at or above standard normal for chronological age and verbal ability.
		Assessment Attitude to reading?
		Ability to read for information?
		Does he read freely for enjoyment?
		Spelling ability?

Throughout the assessment at each stage keep in mind the questions 'What does he know already?' 'What does he need to be taught next?' 'What specific weaknesses does he reveal which may need to be remedied or bypassed?'

PHASE II DEEPER EVALUATION OF PERFORMANCE AT EACH STAGE

STAGE 0

No score on reading test and no evidence of any word recognition skill. Child may lack reading readiness or may have significant perceptual difficulties.

It must be stressed that lack of readiness should not be anticipated as the probable cause of reading failure in non-readers over six and a half to seven years old. This is not to deny that in some individual cases above this age the child may not be ready; intellectual, perceptual and linguistic development may still be at too low a level to permit the child to benefit from instruction in reading. The danger to be guarded against is to assume that 'because Jimmy can't read yet, he can't be ready'. This conclusion, when incorrect, results in a child being occupied with pre-reading activities for a prolonged period when the time could be more profitably spent in beginning reading instruction. Lack of readiness should only be ascertained, and a pre-reading training programme devised, after detailed examination of the selected aspects of the child's performance and behaviour given below; and the question should be kept in mind, 'Do I mean readiness for learning to read by a predominantly "whole-word", *meaning emphasis* approach, or do I mean readiness for a phonic, or *decoding emphasis* approach?'

ASSESSMENT

(Page numbers in parentheses indicate sections in this book where suggestions for training or teaching may be found.)

Q1 Can the child concentrate upon a learning task and listen to the teacher, or is he too distractible and hyperactive?   (p. 94)

Q2 Has the child had adequate language experience and developed adequate speech skills to begin reading? Consider receptive vocabulary, ability to understand teacher's language structure, ability to express himself.   (pp. 100–7)

Q3 Does he seem to be able to grasp that words have unit values in print? Does he realise that the spaces between words have some significance? Can he follow a simple sentence read to him from a book and point to a word then repeated by the teacher? (p. 90)

Q4 Is the child capable of carrying out visual discrimination?

Use Daniels and Diack *Test 4*. Can the child sort and match pictures; simple shapes; letter shapes; word shapes? If the child can successfully match word shapes—in other words, perform well on the final sections of Daniels and Diack *Test 4* or Schonell *Test R7*—there is absolutely no reason why he should not begin to be taught to read by a whole-word method.   (p. 90–1)

Q5 Can he carry out a simple learning task involving the recognition of two words taught from flashcards? Can he do simple picture-word matching after a brief period instruction?   (p. 109)

Q6 Can he co-ordinate hand and eye (visuo-motor co-ordination) sufficiently to copy simple shapes? Can he copy letter shapes? Use Daniels and Diack *Tests 2* and *3*; *and* the copying of the figures presented on page 8. It may also be useful to ask the child to 'draw a man, a house and a tree' to gain some impression of the child's concepts of, and ability to reproduce, these familiar objects. In a clinical situation, the trained diagnostician may use the Bender *Visual-motor Gestalt test* to examine this area of development in more detail.

Hand and eye co-ordination has been overrated in the past as an important prerequisite for reading readiness. Many children whose ability to copy shapes or join dot-to-dot patterns is poor are still capable of learning to read. Poor co-ordination is more important as a problem in the development of writing skills.
(pp. 92–3)

Q7 Has the child developed adequate listening skills to attend to the subtleties of speech sounds within words? This is more important if the early approach to reading is going to stress phonic aspects and simple word-building. The assessment of auditory discrimination will be discussed under STAGE 1.   (pp. 94–7)

N.B. If a child reveals grave visual and visuo-motor perceptual problems the diagnosis may need to be taken to PHASE III, which usually implies specialist assessment by an educational psychologist. Tests used at this level will involve the Bender *Visual-motor Gestalt test*, the Frostig *Developmental test of visual perception*, the Purdue *Perceptual-motor survey*, and the Benton *Visual retention test*. If the child's communication skills in general seem poor the *Illinois test of psycholinguistic abilities* may be given.

A diagnostic programme at PHASE III level is also presented in the book by Tansley.[8] This is likely to be of use to teachers in special school situations rather than the ordinary school setting.

Teachers who are mainly concerned with younger slow learning or perceptually handicapped children are recommended to read the following books and to examine at least one of the tests listed below:

CHAZAN, M. (ed.) (1970) *Reading readiness*, Swansea, University College Publications.

DOWNING, J. and THACKRAY, D. (1971) *Reading readiness*, London, University of London Press.

TANSLEY, A. (1967) *Reading and remedial reading*, London, Routledge.

WEDELL, K. (1973) *Learning and perceptuo-motor disabilities in children*, London and New York, Wiley and Son.

Test material

FROSTIG, M., *et al.* (1964) *Developmental test of visual perception*, Windsor, NFER.

FROSTIG, M., *et al.* (1966) *Programme for training visual perception*, Windsor, NFER.

GATES, A. and MACGINITIE, W. (1968) *Readiness skills test*, Windsor, NFER.

THACKRAY, D. (1974) *Reading readiness profiles*, London, University of London Press.

STAGE 1

Reading ability just measureable. Reading age 5+ to 6+ years according to test used.

Q1 *Basic sight vocabulary* Check the extent of the child's present sight vocabulary of commonly used words. This is done most easily by presenting the first 12, then the next 20 words, from the *Key words list* using separate flashcards for each word. Note the words already known by the child, and also any gaps in his knowledge. The words may be found in the booklet by McNally and Murray (see below), or in the *Teacher's handbook* for the *Ladybird reading scheme* (Wills and Hepworth). (pp. 114–5)

Q2 *Readiness for phonics* A 'readiness for phonics test' is included in the book by Tansley[8] and may be used by any teacher.

In assessing phonic readiness, or in attempting to evaluate a child's present level of development of auditory perception, the following are usually examined:

(a) *Auditory discrimination*

Can the child detect the subtle differences which exist between speech sounds (phonemes)?

It is important to note that one does not expect perfection in the discrimination of speech sounds; indeed, this is not attained until the age of eight years in many normal children, and rather later in slow developers. The purpose in testing auditory discrimination is to make certain that it is adequate for beginning to deal with reading using a phonic method. Where auditory discrimination is very poor it is almost certain to be reflected in very poor articulation in the child's speech.

Difficulty in discriminating speech sounds has frequently been found to be associated with reading problems.[3][9][10] For example to attempt to teach the child that the symbols *v, f,* and *th* have slightly different sounds when a child cannot actually hear the difference is adopting a method which courts confusion.

Auditory discrimination may be assessed using one of the following tests (with a young or very slow learning child a test which embodies picture material is most useful):

Wepman's *Test of auditory discrimination* 40 word-pairs to be judged as same or different when heard by the child. No picture material. (NFER)

J. McLeod and J. Atkinson *Domain phonic survey: sub-test P5* 50 word-pairs to be judged as same or different when heard by the child. No picture material. Part of a very full phonic assessment. (Oliver & Boyd)

Daniels and Diack *Reading test 6* Not possible to give a detailed assessment as the test only samples 12 sounds; but it does use picture material. (Chatto & Windus)

Reed's *Picture hearing test* Very simple to apply. Available from Royal National Institute for the Deaf, Gower Street, London.

If a child's hearing seems at all deficient as revealed by the testing a teacher is strongly advised to refer the individual for specialist examination. For methods and materials to train auditory perception see pages 94–7.

(b) *Sound-blending*

Can the child blend speech sounds heard into meaningful words? This skill has been found extremely important for progress in reading.[10]

Suitable tests for use:

Sub-test 3 in Tansley's book[8.] (Routledge).

Phoneme blending test, D. Moseley.

Sub-test 12 in *The Illinois test of psycholinguistic abilities* (NFER).

The Roswell-Chall *Auditory blending test* (New York, Essay Press).

A teacher who cannot obtain any of these tests can still devise her own material, bearing in mind that she wants to know *how many* sounds presented in sequence can be synthesised by the child; for instance, can he blend two sounds, three sounds, four sounds, g-o, sh-o-p, l-i-tt-le? The tester simply sounds out the word and the child must blend it; reading is not involved.

The child who cannot progress beyond three sounds is likely to have difficulty with word-building.   (p. 122)

(c) *Short-term auditory memory*

The importance of this ability has already been stressed in relationship to oral language development. A very poor auditory memory span can be one reason for failure in sound-blending as described above, and can cause difficulties in word-building and in comprehension. It is usually worth including an assessment of auditory memory span in the diagnosis of reading difficulties.

The standard procedure for the assessment of short-term memory span is to apply a digit repetition test. Such a test should be used as a rough screening procedure, not to attach an exact age level to the child's performance, but to find out if the child's memory span is very much below average for his age. A child who cannot repeat more than 3 or 4 numbers in correct sequence having just heard them may well experience difficulties beyond the elementary stages of word-building; and may, as Moseley[5] points out, have difficulty in processing anything other than very short simple written or printed sentences.

The following test is adequate for the purposes of assessment; the age levels should be regarded as tentative. Three trials are given at each level; that is, if a child fails on the three-digit item in set 1, he is given the three-digit item in set 2, and if he fails that he is given the equivalent item from set 3. Set 1 is used throughout until failure is experienced, then the tester gives second and third tries from sets 2 and 3. The following age levels indicate the point at which most children of that age can succeed with at least one correct repetition out of three trials.

By chronological age 3 years   2 digits
                      4 years   3 digits
                      5 years   4 digits
                  6/7 years   5 digits
                  8/9 years   6 digits
               11 years +   7 digits.

In applying this test one is looking for failure below 4 digits. Present the sequence without rhythm at one digit per ½ second.

Set 1	Set 2	Set 3
7	4	2
3–5	5–7	4–9
6–1–9	2–8–1	3–7–4
4–2–8–3	6–4–3–9	5–8–2–7
5–4–7–9–2	8–1–9–5–7	4–1–8–7–3
8–3–5–2–7–1	5–3–7–6–2–4	9–1–6–5–2–8
5–7–1–9–2–4–8	9–2–8–4–7–1–6	7–3–1–8–2–9–6

If a child has no serious short-term memory deficiency the aim will be to teach him to sound and build words successfully. If a child has a marked deficiency in memory span it will have a bearing on the teaching programme; at times it is one of those deficits which need to be bypassed.   (p. 61, p. 122)

(d) *Basic phonic knowledge*

Check the child's knowledge of common single letter *sounds*. Does he confuse sounds with *names*? Does he confuse (reverse) the letters *b* and *d*? Note any gaps or points of confusion in the child's performance.

Test material is hardly necessary for this assessment since the lower-case letters can be presented on separate cards made by the teacher. However, the following sources may be useful to some teachers:

Daniels and Diack *Test* 5 (Chatto & Windus).
Test PS1 and *PS2* from the *Get reading right* battery, S. Jackson (Gibson). This can be carried out as a *group* assessment if required.

Sub-test 1 from Neale's *Analysis of reading ability* (Macmillan).

A slightly different assessment at a more basic level is to ask the child to point to the correct letter for a sound which you dictate, or to write down the letter which makes that sound.

(pp. 113 and 116)

(e) *Basic word-building skill*

It is desirable to find out if the child can begin to sound out and build words which he has not seen before.

Daniels and Diack Test 7a provides some simple words for this purpose.

The early parts of Schonell's *Test R5* may be used.

Test P1 from the *Domain phonic survey*.

Test PS5 from *Get reading right*.   (pp. 116 and 120)

STAGE 2

Reading age approximately 6 to 7 years.

It is possible for a child to have reached this stage of reading development mainly by a whole-word (look and say) approach; therefore the phonic readiness assessment outlined in STAGE 1 may still be useful here.

Q1 *Basic sight vocabulary* There may be gaps in the child's recognition of the first 100 Key Words (McNally & Murray). Check this over a period of sessions with the child, noting gaps for future teaching.

Q2 *Phonic knowledge* Does he know all the common single-letter sounds? May be worth checking auditory skills as indicated in STAGE 1; judge the need for this on individual merits.

Q3 *Word-building skill* Check the child's ability to analyse and synthesise words. Does he 'sound and build' without being told to do so? Can he do so if encouraged? *How* does he tackle unfamiliar words; has he a system? Has he developed any useful 'phonic sight habits', for instance, does he read the word *string* as *s-t-r-i-n-g* or *str-ing* (the second being by far the more efficient)?

Suitable tests:

Domain phonic tests P1 and *P3*
Get reading right tests PS5/PS6/PS7

Daniels and Diack tests 7b and *7c*

Schonell *Tests R5* and *R6*

Neale's *Analysis sub-test 2*

Also, obtain some insight into the child's word attack skills, use of context, and comprehension from hearing the child read from his book.

Does he read too slowly to gain meaning from the sentences (or too fast)?

Does he tire of the task very quickly?

Does he read with any expression? Does he ignore punctuation?

If child's reading age is near seven years it may be worth applying the Neale *Analysis of reading ability* with particular reference to comprehension and rate.

N.B. Between STAGES 1 and 2 the Doren *Diagnostic reading test* may be particularly useful. It assesses a wide range of skills, including letter recognition, beginning sounds, whole-word recognition, words-within-words, speech consonants, final sounds, blending, rhyming, vowels, sight words and discriminate guessing. Although this test is produced in America it is available to teachers in this country from Education Evaluation Enterprises of Bristol.

STAGE 3

Reading age approximately 7 to 8 years.

Basic phonic skills already developed, or developing. Word attack skills still not fully proficient.

Q1 If it seems necessary, check basic sight vocabulary for any significant gaps.

Q2 *Detailed assessment of phonic knowledge*

(a) If necessary check knowledge of common single-letter sounds.

(b) Assess systematically the child's sight knowledge of the following digraphs and blends. These may each be presented to the child on a separate card:

bl br cl cr dr fl gl gr st ch th sh sp sw pl pr

tr sm sl fr wh sn sk sc tw

spr scr str thr spl squ

There is no significance in the order of presentation.

Note the digraphs or blends which the child has not yet mastered as phonic sight habits.

If a teacher strongly objects to testing phonic sight habits in isolation the same knowledge may be obtained using any of the tests below, which embody the same units within the setting of a real word. It must be pointed out, however, that a child reading a word like *screw* correctly may know that word by sight, but has not generalised the unit *scr* as a sight habit.

Suitable tests:

Domain phonic tests P2, P4

Get reading right PS7/PS8/PS9

Daniels and Diack *Tests 7b, 7c, 7e*

(c) *Word-building skill* Ability to deal with polysyllabic words, or words with common component units. Suitable tests:

Get reading right PS10/PS11

Neale's *Analysis sub-test 3*

Daniels and Diack *Test 7d*

Q3 *Spelling ability*

Suitable tests:

Schonell *Spelling tests S1, S2*

Daniels and Diack *Test 11*

Q4 *Comprehension*

Suitable tests:

Neale's *Analysis of reading ability*

Daniels and Diack *Test 10, 12*

Edinburgh reading test. Select for appropriate age level.

STAGE 4

Reading age 8 to 9+ years.

A reasonable reader (semi-literate) who has reached a temporary plateau or who has specific weaknesses.

Q1 The reading age of 8+ years is not uncommonly followed by a plateau where very little measurable progress is made in spite of frequent reading practice. It is at this stage that the diagnostic technique of *error analysis* is extremely useful.

Listening to children read has always been, and will continue to be, a very important part of the teaching of reading. If we are going to spend valuable time listening to a child read, how may we gain maximum information from the situation? Ideally, if the child reads aloud we should be able to detect any consistent pattern of errors emerging from his performance. This is not easy to do if the child only reads to us occasionally, or if he reads only a very small amount at any one time. We tend to correct his errors as he makes them, and we may help him to develop some system for attacking unfamiliar words; but we don't notice that there is a common pattern of failure running through his word recognition and word-building skills.

Monroe[4] was one of the first reading specialists to recognise the fact that if a child has specific weaknesses in reading they are likely to persist for a very long time unless something is done to remedy the fault and fill the gaps in the child's knowledge. The value of error analysis was also recognised by Neale[6] who developed it as one feature of her test of reading ability.

Before studying the example below it is important to stress that the analysis technique is of little real value with children whose reading ages are low; they will tend to make every type of error at some time. The technique is of maximum value with pupils who have reached a plateau with reading ages between eight plus and nine plus years. It usually highlights exactly where the child is still having difficulties and precisely what needs to be taught.

EXAMPLE

(Child's errors are recorded below the line. The small roman numerals refer to the error category given in Table 1, which follows this extract.)

"Sammy   stopped   and had a look   and   what he
            (*stop*)vi   (*at*)x

saw   made his   head   go round and   round.
(was)s/c iv   (hand)iii   (*around*)v

It   was   a   rickety   old   wooden   bridge
                ref vii   (*wood*)vi   (*drig*)iv/iii

high   up in the   air   over   a river and some
(*h-i-g*)iii   (*a..*)iii   (*off*)ii/vi

of   the   wood   had fallen away so that it was all
                (*woods*)v

on one side. "My head goes round
(*no*)iv (*sid*)i (*hand*)iii (*go*)vi

just when I look at it," cried Sammy miserably.
(*jut*)iii (*said*)x ref vii

"I can't go across there". Mr. Buffin
(*can*)vi (*get*)x ref vii

thought hard. "I'll tell you what we will do.
(*f-f...*)ii (*hand*)iii

We'll cover up your eyes so that you won't see
(*cof*)ii/vi (*eye*)vi

anything. Here's my coat, ... this will do the
(*anybody*)x (*here*)vi

trick."
(*track*)i

So with Mr. Buffin's coat over his boiler
(*B ...*) ref vii (*off*)ii/vi (*d ...*)iv

he steamed back over the
(*st-e ...*)iii (*dack*)iv (*off*)ii/vi

bridge which swayed and creaked in a
(*can't remember*) (*stays*) iii/vi (*crack*)iii/vi

frightening way. Mr. Cornblower and Mr. Buffin
(*th-inking*)iii/xi ref vii (*Boffin*)i

clutched each other as they looked
(*crt-crut*) iii/vi ref iii/vii ref vii (*look*)vi

with horror at the river far below.
(*hor-or*)xi (*f-a-r*)iii (*de ... blow*)iv/vi

(*Note:* s/c = self corrected; ref = refusal)

In order to obtain the sample and collect the errors a story or passage which is probably a little too difficult for the child, and at least 120–150 words long should be selected. Additional information can be added to the analysis table when the child reads from his own book at other times. In sorting the errors into the various caregories below one needs to keep in mind the question, *What is it in the original word that the child has failed to recognise or has rendered incorrectly?*

Table 1. Analysis table

i. Faulty vowel	i/a o/u + silent 'e' rule
ii. Faulty consonant	f/v f/th v/f v/f v/f
iii. Faulty digraphs and blends	–ea– –ea– –dge cr/cl –st –ar– ai? –ea– –ea– –igh st/sw th/fr –ar– oi? –ought?
iv. Reversal	was/saw d/b d/b d/b no/on
v. Sounds added	a– –s
vi. Sounds omitted	–ed –en –er –'t –er –s –s –er –er –ed –ed –ed –e– –es
vii. Refusal	rickety *air* miserably Buffin t*hought boi*ler *e*ach other
viii. Words added	
ix. Words omitted	
x. Contextual guess	at/and cried/said go/get anybody/anything
xi. Unidentified	thinking horror

CONCLUSIONS FROM EXAMINATION OF THE ANALYSIS TABLE

(a) Principal area of difficulty (and therefore area of major instructional need) is concerned with vowel and consonant digraphs and blends. It would be useful with this child to check out fully the phonic sight habits using the digraph and blend cards suggested in STAGE 3 (*Q*2b).   (pp. 114, 119, 122)

(b) The child shows a marked tendency to ignore *word endings* as revealed by category vi.   (p. 120)

(c) A tendency to reverse *b* and *d* and certain 'reversible' words.

A very common difficulty with backward readers. (p. 121)

(d) A certain confusion over the sound-symbol relationship for *v- f-th*. Does this show up also in the child's speech? Is this an auditory discrimination problem?   (p. 49)

Q2 Word Attack Skills
   Suitable tests:
   Get reading right Tests PS10 and PS11.

Q3 Spelling ability
   Suitable tests:
   Schonell *Graded spelling tests S1* or *S2* (Oliver & Boyd).
   Schonell *Graded dictation tests*; or *Tests 1A* and *1B* (Macmillan).

Q4 Comprehension
   Suitable tests:
   Wide span reading test A. Brimer (Nelson). Age Range 7–15 years.
   GAP reading comprehension test J. McLeod and D. Unwin (Heinemann). Covering reading comprehension ages from 7 years 8 months to 12 years 6 months.
   Edinburgh reading test: Stage 2 (University of London Press) or *Stage 3* (Moray House College of Education).
   Neale's *Analysis of reading ability*   (pp. 123–5)

STAGE 5

Reading age above 9½ years.

This can scarcely be regarded as a remedial/diagnostic problem if the child is actually reading up to an adequate age-level.

Q1 However, assessment of comprehension is relevant. Is the child able to read with understanding and with enjoyment? What is his general *attitude* to reading? Is he a *reluctant* rather than an incapable reader? What can we provide to catch his interest?
       (Appendix 6)
   The tests listed for comprehension at STAGE 4 are also suitable here; so are:
NFER *Reading comprehension Test DE* (10–12 years).
NFER *Reading tests EH 1–3* (11–15½ years) (Ginn & Co.).
Edinburgh reading tests: Stage 3, 4, 5 (University of London Press).

Q2 Spelling ability
   Spelling tests listed above for STAGE 4 are suitable here. Specific help in spelling may be needed for certain pupils.   (p. 132–5)

Case studies

1. **David** Chronological age at time of testing 8 years 6 months.
   (i) *Reading level* Reading age 7·2 years (Daniels and Diack *Test 1*).
   (ii) *Verbal intelligence* Verbal IQ 114 (Young's *N.R.I.T.*).
   (iii) *Vocabulary level* Vocabulary equivalent to that of an average nine year-old (Crichton).
   (iv) *Basic sight vocabulary* (*Key words list*) David has a very good grasp of the first 150 words, with the following exceptions:
   off of for—all confused
   what where were when with—all confused
   right—not known at all.
   (v) *Phonic skills*
   (a) all common single-letter sounds known;
   (b) knows most of the common initial consonant digraphs and blends by sight, but some uncertainty with: *sp sk st str spr*. More difficulty with endings, especially *-ng -nd -nk*;
   (c) auditory discrimination (Monroe *Test*)—perfect;
   (d) phoneme blending (Moseley *Test*)—perfect;
   (e) short-term auditory memory (*Digit Span*)—normal for age. Points (c), (d), and (e) indicate that there is absolutely no reason why David should not continue to make progress with a predominantly phonic approach.
   (vi) *Word-building skill* Poor. He lacks system (Schonell *R5*).
   (vii) *Spelling ability* Spelling age 6·8 years (Daniels and Diack *Test 11*). Slightly below reading age, but not markedly so. Some indication of lack of ability, lack of experience, or lack of confidence in applying his existing phonic knowledge to the task of spelling. Some of his errors indicated a possible visual-sequencing difficulty (the correct letters were present but some in wrong order). When David was asked to look at these words afterwards he said that 'They *look* right'. Testing ability in visual sequencing did in fact show him to be rather weak in this process; but this weakness is likely to be helped by some of the general advice given below.
   (viii) *Conclusions* David is typical of the child who has all the necessary sub-skills to make good progress with phonic decoding of unfamiliar words, but fails to make use of his phonic knowledge to any great extent, preferring to cling to look-and-say techniques. His reading errors reveal that he very frequently guesses at new

words from a quick glance at the first letter with some vague help from the context. He makes little use of the information provided by the middle and the ending of a word.

He is reading *Flamingo Book 3* which is just appropriate for his reading level but in general contains too few phonemically regular words for him to experience much success in sounding and building words not already known by sight.

(ix) *Specific advice* Supplement his present scheme with extra work to develop 'word-study techniques'. It may be that a few other children in his class will benefit from such help and they could work as a small group for the following activities. Worksheets or workcards with exercises requiring the child to supply the correct middle vowel or the correct endings of words will help to focus attention on the skill which he needs to develop. The *Brick-Wall Game II* and some of the *Snake Games* from Stott's *Programmed Reading Kit* would fit in well at this stage.

He takes his book home already each evening, could he also take home a few words to learn to read and to spell? About five or six words grouped according to visual or phonemic similarity ('word families') would be helpful, for example, words illustrating the silent *e* rule, or the *ar* unit. I would certainly make use of phonic dictation with this child, not as a *testing* procedure but to train him in careful listening to the temporal order of sounds within words. The material from the word lists taken home would form the basis for such phonic dictation.

(x) *Materials* Alongside the *Flamingo Books* use *The Look Out Gang* (Gibson) from Book 2 to Book 6, since these will provide success with the sounding and building of new words.

Select *suitable* exercises from *Sound Sense* (Arnold), and from the 'c' books in the *Ladybird scheme* from Book 5c onwards. I know that you have the series *Sounds for Reading* (Nisbet) in the school, and the teacher might find some suitable material for word study in the *Teacher's Guidebook* at Level 3.

Several of the *Remedial refresher cards* (Gibson) would be useful work assignments, provided some teaching had preceded each unit.

2. **Shaun** Chronological age at time of testing 9 years 11 months.

(i) *Reading level* Reading age 5·2 years (Daniel and Diack *Test 1*).

(ii) *Verbal intelligence* Not tested owing to lack of time.

(iii) *Non-verbal ability* Performed at average 8 year level (Raven's *Coloured matrices*).

(iv) *Vocabulary level* Level equivalent to that of an average six-year-old (Crichton *Vocabulary* scale).

(v) *Basic sight vocabulary (Key words list)* Very limited. He still does not know *he in is it of that was* from the first dozen words in the list.

(vi) *Visual discrimination* This was assessed because Shaun appeared to experience difficulty in actually *perceiving* the words while reading the *Test 1* and the *Key words list*. Daniels and Diack *Test 4* was used, and apart from two reversals his performance was correct throughout. It might be worth having his vision tested if this has not been done recently, but it is unlikely to prove a major factor in his reading failure.

(vii) *Phonic readiness*

Auditory discrimination. Very poor. This is likely to be a serious problem when taken together with the next deficit (Wepman's *Test*).

Phoneme blending. Very poor. Could not blend even the three-letter words (Moseley's *Test*).

Short-term auditory memory. Only just passed at the 5 year level (*Digit span*).

(viii) *Phonic knowledge*

Shaun does not know with any degree of certainty the following letter sounds *l n u e o g p v y b d.*

(ix) *Word-building skill*

Shows no ability at all in word-building, even after encouragement.

(x) *Conclusions and specific advice*

This boy's general language level is significantly below his non-verbal ability, and the reading deficit is just one symptom of a general backwardness in language skills. His audio-phonic problems indicate that he may need to be taught to break up and build words using larger units than single letters and digraphs. Exercises which will help him to find 'words within words', to recognise syllables by sight, and to study word families may help. I would tend to continue with a predominantly whole-word (look-and-say) approach until he has developed at least a basic sight vocabulary of around 50 words. I strongly recommend a structured use of the language-experience approach in which Shaun will make books connected with his own interests and link writing with reading. As his reading ability improves he can gradually move on to a suitable reading scheme.

It is still necessary to teach him the basic letter sounds which he doesn't know at the moment. Early items from Stott's *Programmed reading kit* will be useful, together with as much phonic teaching from the material produced in his own books as possible. Even though Shaun is almost ten years old the use of flashcards is to be recommended to increase his sight vocabulary.

He is likely to need a great deal of praise and encouragement as well as careful grading of work if he is to experience success. He is already strongly identifying himself with the role of 'reading failure' and sympathetic counselling will be an important part of his remedial therapy.

Suggestions for further study

(a) Carry out the appropriate sequence of diagnostic testing for a backward reader in your class.

(b) Write up the report in the form suggested by the case studies at the end of this chapter.

Always mark such reports CONFIDENTIAL.

Always give the name of the test used, particularly for measuring reading ability, spelling ability, intelligence, etc.

References

1. BOOKBINDER, G. (1970) 'Variations in reading test norms,' *Educational Research*, **12**, 99–105.
2. DANIELS, J. and DIACK, H. (1958) *The Standard reading tests*, London, Chatto & Windus.
3. DEUTSCH, C. (1964) 'Auditory discrimination and learning,' *Merrill-Palmer Qtly*. **10**, 277–96.
4. MONROE, M. (1932) *Children who cannot read*, Chicago, University of Chicago Press.
5. MOSELEY, D. (1973) *Children with special problems*, Milton Keynes, Open University Press.
6. NEALE, M. (1966) *The analysis of reading ability* (2nd Ed.), London, Macmillan.
7. SCHONELL, F. J. (1958) *The essentials of teaching and testing spelling*, London, Macmillan.
8. TANSLEY, A. (1967) *Reading and remedial reading*, London, Routledge.
9. WEPMAN, J. (1959) 'Auditory discrimination, speech, and reading,' *Elementary School Journal*, **60**, 325–33.
10. WESTWOOD, P. (1972) 'Auditory skills and reading progress,' *Remedial Education*, **7**, No. 1, 41–5.
11. YOUNG, D. (1968) *Manual* for *The group reading test*, London, University of London Press.
12. YOUNG, D. and STIRTON, M. (1971) 'Graded word reading test equivalences and reading ages,' *Remedial Education*, **6**, No. 3, 7–8.

Other books and test materials referred to in the text

CONGDON, P. J. (1974) *Phonic skills and their measurement*, Oxford, Blackwell.

DOREN, M. (1956) *Doren diagnostic reading test*, American Guidance Service Inc. Available through Education Evaluation Enterprises, Bristol.

JACKSON, S. (1971) *Get reading right: Phonic tests* and *Teacher's handbook*, Glasgow, Gibson.

McLEOD, J. and ATKINSON, J. (1972) *Domain phonic tests* and *Domain phonic workshop* (worksheets), Edinburgh, Oliver & Boyd.

McNALLY, J. and MURRAY, W. (1968) *Key words to literacy* (2nd Ed.), London, Schoolmaster Publishing Company.

MURRAY, W. (1969) *Teaching reading*, Loughborough, Wills & Hepworth.

SCHONELL, F. J. (1942) *Backwardness in the basic subjects*, Edinburgh, Oliver & Boyd.

SCHONELL, F. J. and SCHONELL, F. E. (1962) *Diagnostic and attainment testing* (4th Ed.), Edinburgh, Oliver & Boyd.

5. The appraisal of written language

Written language is man's highest attainment in verbal symbolization.[7]

This chapter may cause teachers who are zealots for free/creative writing to hold up their hands in horror. It is timely to put in a reminder here that this book is concerned with remedial teaching, and the pupils under consideration are those with learning difficulties.

The able child, and the slow learner who has attained adequate literacy, will find creative writing an essential and purposeful pursuit. For the child with severe difficulties in this area it can be a highly frustrating activity with little reward; much direction from the teacher is vital for such a child in the early stages of writing development, if the activity is to be meaningful and if it is to lead to any progress.

Diagnostic assessment should—but seldom does—extend quite as much into the area of written work as it does to reading and mathematics. Observation of the particular difficulties which a child may have in 'getting his ideas down on paper' is an essential part of diagnostic teaching. Writing ability frequently lags behind progress made in reading because we are less positive and systematic in our teaching in this area.

Very little has been provided for the teacher in the way of normative data on appropriate levels of performance in written work to be expected at given age levels. Many years ago Burt,[2] and later Schonell,[13 15] gave samples of compositions considered 'typical' for pupils in the age range seven to thirteen or fourteen years; but even at the time they could have been only at best a very rough guide. Burt quite rightly pointed out in the 1920s, 'Of all school subjects English composition is one in which individual variation is widest' (p. 435).[2] Schonell devised a scoring system for compositions based on (a) content, (b) structure, (c) accuracy. Burt gave norms for such measures as (a) length of essay, (b) average length of sentence, (c) quality. It is extremely doubtful whether these norms would have any bearing on present-day standards with greater and earlier emphasis placed upon creative writing. However, the four chapters devoted by Schonell[13] to written English are still very useful reading.

Myklebust[78] provides the only recent normative data on the written language of individuals aged between seven and seventeen years; and these are based on the results of children working on the *Picture story language test*.[7] In this test a standard procedure is adopted which requires the pupil to write as much as he can about a stimulus picture which shows a boy arranging miniature furniture and figures on a table top. The test can be used with small groups, and usually takes approximately twenty to thirty minutes to administer. Since the norms relate to American populations they need to be viewed with some degree of caution if the test is used with other ethnic groups.

Picture material can be used to stimulate written work even if norms are not consulted. If the aim is to obtain a reasonably objective assessment of what the child *can* write unaided the picture would be presented without discussion (unlike a *teaching* situation).

If we observe the difficulties which some pupils exhibit when left to produce free writing unaided they may be summarised under the following headings:

(i) problems in *organisation* of the content; inability to state clearly in a logical order the points to be made in a story, description, or factual account;

(ii) a very *restricted vocabulary* which limits the possible range of expression. The actual vocabulary used in writing may appear even more restricted than the child's oral vocabulary owing to inhibitions about spelling; the child is stuck with the words he thinks he can spell;

(iii) a very *restricted range of sentence structure*;

(iv) difficulties with *grammatical accuracy*;

(v) difficulties with *spelling*;

(vi) difficulties with *handwriting*;

(vii) lack of *interest and motivation*; very little produced; no sense of satisfaction.

All these features can be observed reasonably objectively, and each has implications for teaching.

If a teacher is concerned with items (i) to (iv) above, it will obviously be necessary to obtain a sample of written expression in a 'freewriting' situation. The sample is then evaluated (albeit sub-jectively) to discover the extent to which a child cannot yet organise his ideas, has a limited expressive vocabulary (especially a lack of adjectives, adverbs, and prepositions), and has a stilted and over-used sentence pattern to serve all purposes. If, however, the teacher is concerned with spelling or handwriting the relevant information could be obtained from a group through the use of dictation passages. Suitable material is provided by Schonell[14] and Peters.[10]

In general, it is obviously unreasonable to expect the standard of written work to be above the level of reading ability, and a child's reading age should be taken into account when evaluating a sample of written English. *Breakthrough to Literacy* (Longman) and other language-experience approaches to reading, which encourage early writing to reinforce reading skills, are likely to develop the confidence to use a greater variety of sentence structures in written language. These approaches are described in detail later in this book.

Teachers of less able children frequently ask 'How fully should I mark their written work? Should all errors be pointed out and corrected?'

The first point to make is that if the advice concerning 'freely guided writing' as opposed to 'free writing' in chapter 11 is followed the number of mistakes made by the child will be much smaller, and marking is less of a harrowing experience. The second point is that there will be times when one doesn't correct work at all. For example, it would be pedantic in the extreme to mark the notes made by a less able child while on an outside visit (see page 69), or at school camp, or in first writing the plot for a little story or play; on the other hand, this kind of material can reveal much about the child's level of development in written language. Finally, expect a child to correct only those words which it is reasonable that he should know relative to his reading ability, and which he needs frequently in his written work. In general, err on the side of leniency since over-marking a child's work can appear as rejection of the sometimes considerable efforts made by him. Williams[17] makes the point, 'The slow learner cannot readily find associations between the crimson strictures across his writing and yesterday's thoughts and feel-ing that it represented' (p. 131).

If a child's written work seems very poor, Myklebust[7][8] suggests that the teacher consider whether the disability stems from lack of training and experience, a defect in spoken language, backwardness in reading, or from a specific disability, which in its extreme form is usually referred to as *dysgraphia*[4][18] (in the same way that a specific and extreme form of reading disability may be referred to as *dyslexia*). Acute difficulties with writing and spelling are frequently associated with genuine cases of dyslexia.[5]

Spelling

In the matter of spelling pupils seem to fall into one of three main groups: (a) those who without conscious effort appear to develop spelling 'insight' through their normal auditory-visual experience of language, (b) those who do need some form of regular help in order to develop this insight, and (c) those who spell so badly even in relationship to their reading ability that their problem is obviously due to a definite, and sometimes specific, disability in this field. Pupils falling into one of the last two categories are not confined to the least able groups or classes; nor are they necessarily very poor readers.

Factors associated with spelling disability appear to be:

(i) Low functional verbal intelligence, meagre vocabulary and a poor level of language development;

(ii) Poor reading ability;

(iii) Weak powers of visual imagery and recall;

(iv) Over-dependence upon *phonic* aspects—'stayshun'; 'thay'; 'sed'—(as Peters[11] states, 'spelling depends on visual, not auditory imagery. To sound out a word is to court confusion' p. 78);

(v) Dependence upon visual pattern without checking against sound values within the word; correct letters may be there but in the wrong order, child will say the word 'looks all right'; this may also indicate poor visual sequencing ability;

(vi) Faulty visual habits, careless attention to detail, poor directional attack in reading and a tendency to reverse;

(vii) Speech defects and poor articulation—is he saying the word correctly?

(viii) Auditory problems (especially auditory discrimination)—is he hearing the word correctly?

(ix) Poor sound blending ability;

(x) Emotional and temperamental attitude—does he care in the slightest whether or not he can spell? Has he already identified with the role of 'poor speller'?

Accurate diagnosis is often difficult, particularly since it is quite common for one pupil to be subject to several of the above difficulties. Within a remedial situation it is usual to carry out a careful analysis of a child's actual spelling errors to determine what form of word study help is likely to be of benefit. Such analysis can be performed on the errors made in several paragraphs of dictated material, supplemented by information from the mistakes in the child's free writing.

The following categories have been found useful in the analysis of spelling errors:

Reasonable phonic alternative
Transposition of letters
Omission of letters
Insertion of letters
Consonant error (including digraphs/blends)
Vowel error (including digraphs)
Reversals
Single/double letter errors
Repetition of letters or syllables
Unrecognisable letter shape.

The whole topic of error analysis is well covered by Peters.[9] [11] She goes on to suggest that the main priorities in the teaching and remediation of spelling are to develop an awareness of common letter sequencies, to train the child in habits of 'careful looking' when dealing with word shapes, to teach correct letter formation leading to easy and swift handwriting and, finally, to improve the child's self-image. Observation of the very laboured efforts of the adult illiterate in spelling quite simple words shows how lack of familiarity and practice in writing has prevented what to most individuals has become a 'habit' response: the more a person writes (and spells correctly) the less thought has to be centred on the task of spelling. 'Before spelling can become habitual, that is, completely automatised, it has to go through the process of skill learning' (p. 75).[10]

Useful material for testing spelling has been described in the sections dealing with reading. The tests are repeated here without description.

Graded spelling test 11, J. Daniels and H. Diack (Chatto & Windus).

Graded spelling tests, F. J. Schonell (Oliver & Boyd).

Diagnostic tests of spelling, S4, S5, S6, F. J. Schonell.[13]

Spelling test 1A (irregular words), Spelling test 1B (regular words).

and *Graded dictation tests A to F*, F. J. Schonell.[14]

Graded spelling test and dictation passages, M. Peters.[10]

Samples

The samples presented here are fairly typical. The reader is referred to a publication by Cotterell[3] where other examples are provided and interpreted.

1. **John K** Chronological age 12 years 6 months. Reading age 8·4 years (Schonell *R1*). Spelling age 6·3 years (Schonell *S1*).

today we went to the *ipswich museum** and we sor a lote of
finsy and the man sed Dont tuchr and we sor the debroom
and the fat man sed Dont linr on the polichd fonuch and i haD
a God timr we wenD to see the Duksr and we gavr the Duksr
the Pecos of Breb that we Did not wont Befo we wendt t homr
we plad hidsnsek and climir the theres

(No punctuation used throughout.)

Translation

Today we went to the Ipswich Museum, and we saw a lot of things. And the man said, 'Don't touch'. And we saw the bedroom, and the fat man said, 'Don't lean on the polished furniture'. And I had a good time. We went to see the ducks and we gave the ducks the pieces of bread that we did not want. Before we went home we played hide-and-seek and climbed the trees.

Consider (i) the marked discrepancy between reading ability and spelling ability; (ii) organisation of the material; (iii) the types of error made; (iv) the frequent use of the capital *D* rather than the lower case *d*; (v) the frequent use of *and*.

---

* Indicates two words already written on the cover of the boy's booklet and therefore copied.

2. **Sidney R** Chronological age 11 years 8 months. Reading age 7 years 2 months (test not recorded). Spelling age 6·8 years.

> are glassroom is small but it is all rot begoss there is owy 17 of
> us in have we have got to doors difre tichig mshes an a
> tip rotre we have a lot of piches on the wall a decplan of
> holday looklets we allso have are one loges.

Translation

Our classroom is small but it is all right because there is only 17 of us. In here we have got two doors, different teaching machines, and a typewriter. We have a lot of pictures on the wall (and) a display of holiday booklets. We also have our own lockers.

Consider (i) some of the points listed for John K. (above); (ii) the possible reason for writing such errors as 'glassroom' for 'classroom'.

3. **John F** Chronological age 22 years. Reading age not recorded, but had previously been an adult illiterate. This work (unaided) produced after eight months of instruction.

A PARTY

> There was anacotmen off noises† comeing from the houes
> noitheing was panelea earabull hepst some musc
> Has I walt in throow the door the musc grow lowder and
> lowder the noises mor destingweshed now everyon was enjying
> the dancing the danc floor was cerowed there was lights
> flashing† on and off withe the beet of the musc
> and the foor it sellf seemd to be in rifoem withe the musc
> the room was vere hot and you needed a drink
> The hous was decoraed withe colourd poster of vaimers
> pop singer and colourd fiml shos on pojecktiod on the walls
> ther was refreshment†

Translation

There was an assortment of noises coming from the house. Nothing was plainly audible except some music.

As I walked in through the door the music grew louder and louder, the noises more distinguished. Now everyone was enjoying the dancing. The dance-floor was crowded. There were lights flashing on and off with the beat of the music; and the floor itself seemed to

† These words copied.

be in rhythm with the music. The room was very hot and you needed a drink.

The house was decorated with coloured posters of famous pop singers, and coloured film shows projected on the walls. There was refreshment.

Other examples of this man's errors taken from different material: Tsoport = *Stockport*; egorcason = *education*; fyou = *few*; quast = *just*; worlk = *work*; mennea = *many*; maicks shour = *makes sure*; pepol, pelpoe, peploe = *people*.

4. **Thomas H** Chronological age 15 years 7 months. Reading age 6·9 years (Schonell *R1*). Spelling age 7·3 years (Daniels and Diack *11*).

When itis nili christmas, I think that all the apens that you give to under poeple and your sefr. It was a gofoe moment when Jeisa was bon they selled bret when the new msiaer is her that why we sellib bret. And we think has christmas shild be geting drucer, them you will mise the apens, the children presand then you will think that christmas is senlding you money all the times. You can have a good christmas with out get drucer I men wot the pot of geting druc. You colud have a fuyou drink. But dot sedn you money on think your children dot wont at all. Thay is no yous in bing your children think they dot wont at all. Wot I do is let them have wot they wont then eive boyd is apee. Then no body can sa that it was a bad christmas at all last year you be ebo to go to chersh.

Translation

When it is nearly Christmas I think that all the happiness that you give to other people and yourself. It was a joyful moment when Jesus was born. They celebrate when the new Messiah is here, that [is] why we celebrate. And we think at Christmas should be getting drunk. Then you will miss the happiness, the children's presents, and then you will think that Christmas is spending your money all the time. You can have a good Christmas without getting drunk, I mean, what's the point of getting drunk. You could have a few drinks but don't spend your money on things your children don't want at all. There is no use in buying your children things they don't want at all. What I'd do is let them have what they want then everybody is happy. Then nobody can say that it was a bad Christmas at all last year. You be able to go to church.

Handwriting

Examination of the handwriting of children in the bottom streams of most secondary schools shows that handwriting is a skill which has been imperfectly acquired by very many slow learners. A child of high academic ability may have specific difficulty with handwriting. At times, poor handwriting is symptomatic of poor motor co-ordination; and poor co-ordination is found in a few very able children as well as slow learners.

There is no doubt that correct letter formation needs to be taught, particularly to those children with problems of co-ordination.[16]

Poor handwriting can be a handicap for the able child following an academic course, since subject specialists may judge a child's ability in their subject from the quality of his written work. Briggs[1] found some evidence to indicate that standards of handwriting (legibility and style) do influence the assessment of essays.

In terms of diagnostic assessment a teacher must observe at first hand how a child forms his letters. Many slow learners have been left to pick up the most inefficient methods for forming letters. Consider the position of the child's hand and arm, his sitting posture, and the position of the paper. Observe how he holds the writing instrument. Consider, 'Should he be using this *style* of handwriting, or is it causing particular difficulties?'

Some advice on training is given in a later section of this book. Two articles by Presland[12] will be found useful.

Suggestions for further study

(a) Use the error categories suggested on page 68 and analyse the mistakes made in example (3) **John F.** What specific difficulties can you find to direct the teaching of this man from this stage in his development?

(b) Give the composition titles 'Home' and 'If I had wings and could fly' to a class containing pupils within the age ranges eight to nine or eleven to twelve years. Arrange the finished material in order of merit and find the essay which comes half way down the distribution (the median sample). Compare it with those provided by Schonell.[15] What are your conclusions? The maximum time allowed for writing the composition should be thirty minutes. No discussion should precede the writing, and no help with spelling or vocabulary should be given.

References

1. BRIGGS, D. (1970) 'The influence of handwriting on assessment,' *Educational Research*, **13**, 50–5.
2. BURT, C. (1962) *Mental and scholastic tests* (4th Ed.), London, Staples Press.
3. COTTERELL, G. (1973) *Diagnosis in the classroom*, Centre for the Teaching of Reading, University of Reading.
4. JORDAN, D. (1972) *Dyslexia in the classroom*, Columbus, Ohio, Merrill Publishing Co.
5. MILES, T. R. (1970) *On helping the dyslexic child*, London, Methuen.
6. MOSELEY, D. (1969) 'The talking typewriter and remedial teaching in a secondary school,' *Remedial Education*, **4**, No. 4, 196–202.
7. MYKLEBUST, H. (1965) *Development and disorders of written language*, Vol. I.
8. MYKLEBUST, H. (1973) *Development and disorders of written language*, Vol. II, London and New York, Grune & Stratton.
9. PETERS, M. (1967) *Spelling: caught or taught?* London, Routledge.
10. PETERS, M. (1970) *Success in spelling*, Cambridge Institute of Education Press.
11. PETERS, M. (1970) 'The teaching of spelling,' *Remedial Education*, **5**, No. 2, 76–9.
12. PRESLAND, J. (1971) 'A psychologist's approach to backwardness in handwriting,' *Remedial Education*, **6**, Nos. 1 and 2 (two articles).
13. SCHONELL, F. J. (1948) *Backwardness in the basic subjects*, Edinburgh, Oliver & Boyd.
14. SCHONELL, F. J. (1958) *The essentials of teaching and testing spelling*, London, Macmillan.
15. SCHONELL, F. J. and SCHONELL, F. E. (1960) *Diagnostic and attainment testing* (4th Ed.), Edinburgh, Oliver & Boyd.
16. WEDELL, K. (1973) *Learning and perceptuo-motor disabilities in children*, London and New York, Wiley & Sons.
17. WILLIAMS, A. A. (1970) *Basic subjects for the slow learner*, London, Methuen.
18. WOLFF, A. (1970) 'Dysgraphia,' *Remedial Education*, **5**, No. 2, 72–5.

Recommended Reading

PETERS, M. L. (1975) *Diagnostic and Remedial Spelling Manual* London, Macmillan.
WADE, B. & WEDELL, K. (eds) (1974) *Spelling: Task and Learner* University of Birmingham Press.
MARTIN, N. *et al* (1976) *Writing and Learning Across the Curriculum 11–16* London, Ward Lock.

6. The assessment of number skills

The scope of this section is deliberately limited; to attempt to cover all aspects of mathematics is impossible in a volume this size. We are concerned here mainly with number work and arithmetic. The tests listed in the final part of the chapter indicate some measures which are available for wider assessment.

It is generally agreed that a slow learning child, or a child with specific difficulties in the field of number/mathematics, needs longer to acquire and assimilate a particular operation or concept; he requires the same basic process or operation presented in a variety of ways to aid generalisation.[10] There may be every reason to lower the sights for the least able children, and concentrate in the early stages on teaching more thoroughly a limited number of basic concepts and the mastery of certain skills. Attempting to teach some aspects of mathematics to children without these basic skills and concepts is akin to building a house without foundations. 'Teaching must be so systematic and graded that the child also becomes more and more aware of what the number system is and how it can help in ordering the quantitative aspects of his environment' (p. 149).[11]

The remedial teacher may be faced with a child who has failed in number/mathematics usually for one or more of the following reasons:

(i) At some stage in his development the teacher's pacing of the work has outstripped his ability to master fully and assimilate the processes involved, or there was so little structuring of a 'discovery mathematics' situation that he failed to abstract anything whatsoever from it.

(ii) The teacher's use of language in explaining number and mathematical relationships did not match the child's level of comprehension. The child lacked the ability to internalise the material verbally.

(iii) Abstract symbols were introduced too early in the absence of concrete materials or real-life situations, or concrete materials and meaningful situations were removed too soon. As Lovell has said, 'In some mathematical curricula it would seem that there is an attempt to force abstraction in pupils ... there is a danger that if mathematical ideas too advanced for their thinking skills and experience are forced on children they will either assimilate them with distortion or turn away from them in distaste' (p. 17).[7]

(iv) The child's grasp of simple number relationships was not fully developed before larger numbers involving complications of place-value, etc., were introduced.

(v) The use of one particular type of structural apparatus was over-stressed, and learning became too specific to permit generalisation to other situations.

(vi) The child may have visual perceptual problems which have caused difficulties in appreciating pattern, configuration, accuracy in counting, and the correct position of number symbols (47 being confused with 74, etc.).[3][13]

(vii) The child may also have reading difficulties and, therefore, have been condemned to a diet of 'sum cards' because he couldn't read the problems on the assignment sheets. Teaching only a set of computational tricks does not amount to efficient teaching; such tricks are usually rapidly forgotten since they do not constitute meaningful learning.

With modern approaches to the teaching of basic number work and mathematics the need for regular assessment of individual progress is greater than ever before. Periodic checks on the child's understanding of these new activities are essential; and such checks usually involve individual questioning and demonstration. 'Without this the teacher has little idea whether the pupil carries out an activity in rote fashion, through the help of other children, or with partial or complete understanding' (p. 189).[7] The point is also well made by Brissenden,[2] 'Keeping track of their complex network of learning paths is a much greater challenge to the teacher than is the traditional pattern in which he needs only to record the place each child has reached in a sequence which all are following' (p. 117). Teachers faced with the need for such individual assessment procedures may find the Nuffield Mathematics Project Guides *Check up I* and *II*, the book by Fogelman,[6] Appendix 7 of *Mathematics in Primary Schools*[9] and the *Number readiness test* in Eileen Churchill's book[4] all useful source material.

Diagnostic programme

As with reading, the diagnosis of number difficulties should amount to the asking of a series of relevant questions in order to discover a child's present level of achievement and detect any areas of significant weakness. The answers to the questions should yield direct information for teaching.

As in the diagnostic assessment of reading, writing and spelling so, too, in the case of number it is vitally important to observe *how* a child tackles a particular task.

Phase I

Apply a suitable number/mathematics attainment test to determine the child's present functional level.

Suitable tests may be selected from:

Leicester number test (revised edition) by W. Gillham and K. Hesse (University of London Press). Norms to cover the age range 7+ to 9 years.

Nottingham number test by W. Gillham and K. Hesse (University of London Press). Norms to cover the age range 9+ to 11 years.

Both the above tests are designed to assess understanding of basic concepts of the number system and grasp of computation. The tests can be administered orally to groups of children, and can also be used *diagnostically* with individuals even if their age falls outside the stated range.

Group mathematics test by D. Young (University of London Press). This test is very suitable for children from a wide ability range in the 6½ to 8½ years age group, and also for slow learners up to the age of 13 years. No reading is involved as the test is orally administered. Two forms of the test are available for simultaneous administration to large groups.

Graded arithmetic-mathematics test (Decimal version) by P. Vernon (University of London Press).

This rather steeply graded test gives arithmetic-mathematics ages from 7 to 21 years. It is suitable for screening and coarse assessment at secondary school level.

Mathematics attainment test A (Ginn for N.F.E.R.). Test No. 231. Manual 231A. The test was standardised in 1969/71 and provides scores for children in the age range 7–8½ years. It contains 42 items, is orally administered, and takes approximately 40 minutes to work. The material contained in the test covers a fairly wide range of topics (shape, graphs, estimation, etc.). Although the test does not involve reading it places fairly heavy demands on listening skills. Coefficient of reliability = ·94.

Mathematics attainment test B (Ginn for N.F.E.R.). Test No. 191. Manual 191A. Standardised in 1965 this test covers the age range 8 years 6 months to 9 years 8 months. Oral administration takes approximately 45 minutes. Coefficient of reliability = ·92.

A.P.U. Arithmetic Test (Hodder & Stoughton). This test produced in 1976 is very suitable for initial screening in the age range 11 to 18 years. Coefficient of reliability = ·95.

For N.F.E.R. tests for the older age ranges see final section of this chapter.

Phase II

If the child's performance on the first test is very poor consider the following points. At this stage almost all the assessments will need to be made with individual children and using appropriate concrete materials, number symbol cards, etc.

(i) Check the child's grasp of the *vocabulary* associated with number skills. (See Appendix 1.)

(ii) Check the child's grasp of *conservation of number*.

(iii) Can the child sort objects given *one attribute* (for example, shape, colour or size, etc.)?

(iv) Can the child sort given *two attributes* (for example, colour and shape, etc.)?

(v) Can the child match a given group of objects up to ten by *one-to-one-matching*?

(vi) Can the child *count* correctly actual objects to ten? to twenty?

(vii) Can the child *recognise number symbols* to ten? to twenty?

(viii) Can the child place the *number symbols in correct sequence* to ten? to twenty?

(ix) Can the child *write numbers* correctly from dictation (random order of presentation)? to ten? to twenty?

(x) Can the child arrange objects (or structural apparatus) in *order of size*?

(xi) Has the child any grasp of *ordinal value* (fifth, tenth, etc.)?

(xii) Can the child perform *simple addition and subtraction with numbers below ten in a written form*? With or without apparatus, finger-counting, tally marks, etc.?

(xiii) Can the child '*count on*' in a simple addition situation?

(xiv) Can the child recognise coins and paper money? $\frac{1}{2}$p 1p 2p 5p 10p 50p £1?

PHASE III

If the child's performance on the first test was slightly better, or if he is able to succeed with most of the material in PHASE II above, consider the following:

(i) Can the child carry out *simple addition* with numbers below ten and totals below 20? Does he do this easily and without finger-counting? (See *One minute addition test* below.) Can he do the same thing when the symbols represent small sums of money? Does he appear to know his *number bonds* as correct habit responses?

(ii) Can he carry out *simple subtraction* as above? (See *One minute subtraction test* below.) Is there a marked difference between his performance in addition and subtraction?

(iii) How does he tackle the *written forms* of addition and subtraction? Is he tied to one form of recording or 'sum', that is, to vertical or horizontal presentation of figures:

$$\begin{array}{r} 3 \\ +5 \\ \hline \end{array} \quad \text{or} \quad 3+5= \qquad ?$$

(iv) Has the child grasped the *commutative law* in addition (that the *order* of items to be totalled does not matter). Does he, for example, see at once that $5+3$ and $3+5$ are bound to give the same total?

(v) Does the child understand *additive composition* (all the possible ways of producing a given set or total); for example, that 5 is $4+1$, $3+2$, $2+3$, $1+4$, $5+0$, etc.?

(vi) Does the child understand the *complementary* or *revisible character* of addition and subtraction $(7+3=10.$ $10-7=3.$ $10-3=7,$ etc.)?

(vii) Can a child watch an operation demonstrated using concrete material and then write it down in number form?

(viii) Can a child translate a written form of 'sum' into a practical demonstration (the reverse of (vii) above)?

(ix) Can the child listen to a real-life situation described to him in words and then work out the problem for himself in written form? (For example, seven people were waiting at the bus stop. When the bus came only three could get on. How many were left to wait for the next bus?) Use numbers below 20.

(x) Can the child recognise and/or write from dictation numbers up to 50?

(xi) Can he tell the time to the nearest hour and half-hour?

(xii) Does he know the days of the week? The months of the year?

PHASE IV

If the child is able to succeed with most of the early items in the first test, or if he seems reasonably competent in many of the areas examined above, then consider:

(i) Can the child read and write numbers to 100? to 1000? Can he read and write correctly larger sums of money (for example, 'The car costs £843'; does he write '80043£')?

(ii) Can the child quickly write down a number which is 'three more than' or 'four more than' a given number? Check particularly when this involves a change from less than 100 to more than a 100 (for instance, 'What number is 5 more than 98')?

(iii) Does the child understand place value? With tens and units? With hundreds tens and units?

(iv) Does the child understand place value as it relates to addition?

(v) What method does the child use for subtraction of H.T.U.?

(vi) Can the child recognise fractions, $\frac{1}{2}$ $1\frac{1}{2}$ $\frac{1}{4}$ $\frac{3}{4}$ $6\frac{3}{4}$ $\frac{1}{10}$ ·3 etc.?

(vii) Can the child *halve* and/or *double* numbers mentally?

(viii) Does he know his 'tables'?

(ix) Can he add money mentally and give change by 'counting on'?

(x) Can the child use a ruler to measure and construct lines?

(xi) Can the child carry out *multiplication*? To what level of understanding?

(xii) Can the child carry out *division*? To what level of understanding?

(xiii) Can the child tell the time accurately and solve simple problems involving time?

In general, and at all levels, does the child appear to have been taught tricks of computation which are rapidly forgotten as soon as the material changes or the skill is not practised?

One minute addition and *One minute subtraction tests*

Many years ago Ballard[1] devised a *One minute oral addition test* and a *One minute oral subtraction test,* and provided norms for the age ranges 5 to 12/13 years. These tests required individual administration. Vernon[12] provided some tentative revision of the norms in 1949.

The tests printed below are designed for group administration and were standardised on a representative sample of 1,894 children in the age range five plus to eleven years from fourteen primary schools in the north–west of England. Norms are provided in Appendix 3. Coefficients of Reliability (test/retest): ·92 addition; ·89 subtraction. The tests may be reproduced without infringing copyright. The items should be typed or written clearly on the sheet of paper upon which the child writes his answers: *they must not be written up on the blackboard.*

It is advisable to use rather wider spacing between the lines if young children are being tested. If the method of recording used in the school is different from that shown on the paper it may be necessary either to write the items in that form (for example, 4, 3 → 7); or (as was done in the standardisation sample) to give some initial practice in the type of sum presented here.

These instructions should be followed if use is to be made of the norms provided. Give out the printed answer sheets, placing the paper face down on the desk; the child writes his name on the back of the sheet (the teacher will later write the child's chronological age to the nearest half-year next to the name).

Say, 'Turn over your papers now. You see the adding sums? It says ADDITION at the top.' (It is permissible to use terminology familiar to the children; if *adding* and *addition*, *take away* and *subtract* are not known or used, substitute suitable terms.) 'When I say START you are to do as many sums as you can until I say STOP. Write your answers at the side of each sum. Ready? START now.' After exactly one minute say, 'STOP. Pencils down.' Make sure that every child does stop writing. 'Well done: that was very good. Now we are going to do the take away sums, the SUBTRACTION sums for one minute. Pick up your pencil. Don't forget these are *take away* sums, don't add them. All ready? START now.' After exactly one minute say 'STOP. Pencils down.' Make sure that every child does stop. Collect in papers for marking.

ADDITION		SUBTRACTION	
$2 + 1 =$	$6 + 3 =$	$2 - 1 =$	$8 - 5 =$
$1 + 4 =$	$5 + 5 =$	$5 - 1 =$	$9 - 5 =$
$2 + 2 =$	$6 + 2 =$	$3 - 2 =$	$10 - 4 =$
$4 + 2 =$	$2 + 7 =$	$5 - 3 =$	$9 - 4 =$
$3 + 4 =$	$4 + 6 =$	$6 - 2 =$	$10 - 3 =$
$2 + 3 =$	$5 + 7 =$	$2 - 2 =$	$11 - 2 =$
$5 + 2 =$	$8 + 3 =$	$6 - 4 =$	$10 - 6 =$
$4 + 5 =$	$4 + 9 =$	$7 - 2 =$	$12 - 3 =$
$3 + 5 =$	$7 + 6 =$	$6 - 1 =$	$12 - 6 =$
$2 + 8 =$	$8 + 6 =$	$7 - 3 =$	$11 - 5 =$
$4 + 4 =$	$9 + 8 =$	$8 - 2 =$	$13 - 3 =$
$2 + 5 =$	$6 + 9 =$	$7 - 5 =$	$12 - 9 =$
$1 + 8 =$	$8 + 7 =$	$8 - 3 =$	$14 - 6 =$
$6 + 4 =$	$9 + 5 =$	$7 - 4 =$	$17 - 8 =$
$3 + 7 =$	$9 + 7 =$	$9 - 3 =$	$16 - 9 =$

The two books by Schonell are still of some value here, although current trends in the teaching of mathematics have moved a long way from regarding arithmetic as an end in itself. (*Diagnosis and remedial teaching in arithmetic*, 1957, and *Diagnostic and attainment testing*, 4th Ed., 1960, Oliver & Boyd.)

Clarke[5] suggested that in addition to assessing computational skills in arithmetic a complete evaluation of performance will involve consideration of levels of understanding, concept formation, attitudes to the subject, interest and study habits.

The National Foundation for Educational Research has produced a useful series of semi-diagnostic tests under the titles *Basic mathematics tests A, B,* and *C* (ordered as *Tests 256, 257,* and *252* respectively). These are published by Ginn. The first two tests, *A* and *B*, cover the age ranges seven to eight years and eight to nine years, and are orally administered. A recording grid in the test booklet allows some interpretation of which processes and concepts have been mastered or are still to be mastered by the child. *Test C* is for the nine to ten and a half year old age group and does require reading ability in the child. The tests can be used diagnostically outside the prescribed age ranges.

The remaining tests summarised here are mainly for the assessment of attainment levels in mathematics. The Head of Remedial Department or Head of Mathematics may find them useful for average and above average children. All require reading ability on the part of the child, and all take from forty-five minutes to an hour to administer.

Mathematics attainment test C1 (formerly *Junior maths test C1*), published by Ginn for N.F.E.R. (Test 190, Manual 190A.) Standardised 1965. Age range 9+ to 10+ years. Covers graphs, simple geometry, base, series, fractions, arithmetical processes and equations.

Mathematics attainment test C3 (Decimal version), published by Ginn for N.F.E.R. Age range 9+ to 10+ years. Covers computation, metric measures, graphs, fractions, time. (Test 215, Manual 215A.)

Mathematics attainment test DE1 (Test 253, Manual 253A). Age range 10–12 years.

Mathematics attainment test DE2 (Test 228, Manual 228A). Age range 10–12 years.

Mathematics attainment test EF (Test 263). Age range 11 years 11 months–13+ years. Also required for this test: *Answer sheets* 263B, *Marking key* 263C, *Manual*.

The Coefficient of Reliability is above ·90 for all these tests.

Bristol achievement tests: Mathematics (Thomas Nelson), 1969.

These tests are well designed to assess aspects of mathematics emphasised in most modern curriculum development programmes. The five sections of each test are concerned with number, reasoning, space, measurement, arithmetic and algebraic laws and conventions. Good reading ability is required.

Level I (Forms A & B) 8 years–9 years 11 months. Level II (Forms A & B) 9 years–10 years 11 months. Level III (Forms A & B) 10 years–11 years 11 months.

The following items may also be useful within the diagnosis/remediation context:

Concept assessment kit: conservation, M. Goldschmid and P. Bentler. (1968, Educational and Industrial Testing Service). Details from N.F.E.R. Test Agency.

Evaluating pupils' understanding of arithmetic, W. H. Dutton (1964, Prentice-Hall).

Chapter VII in *Learning disabilities* by D. J. Johnson and H. R. Myklebust (1967, Grune & Stratton and Heinemann).

Suggestions for further study

(a) Examine critically at least one of the following: the *Leicester number test*, the *Nottingham number test*, Young's *Group mathematics test,* one of the N.F.E.R. *Mathematics attainment tests A, B,* or *C* or the *Basic mathematics tests A, B,* or *C.*

Consider in particular the vocabulary and the sentence structure used in the orally-administered items. Suggest possible improvements.

(b) If a child is very poor in number work it is commonly considered that a check should be made of his grasp of conservation of number and of continuous quantities (e.g. liquid or plasticine). Study some of the methods for assessing conservation (the books referred to on page 75 may help). Try some of the experiments with at least one of your backward children. To what extent do you find that your use of language in questioning the child influences his responses? What are the implications?

(c) Apply the *One minute addition* and *subtraction tests* to a class of junior children. After marking the answer-strips arrange the sheets in rank order. Compare the order with that obtained from any other test of mathematical ability applied to the class, and with your own subjective impressions of the children's levels of ability in computation.

(d) Examine the *Yardsticks* series of criterion—referenced tests in mathematics (Nelson, 1975).

References

1. BALLARD, P. B. (1933) *The new examiner,* London, University of London Press.
2. BRISSENDEN, T. H. (1972) 'Deciding the objectives of primary mathematics' in Chazan, M. (ed.), *Aspects of primary education,* Cardiff, University Press.
3. CAWLEY, N. (1972) 'Diagnosing difficulties in number,' *Remedial Education,* **7**, No. 3, 29–32.
4. CHURCHILL, E. (1961) *Counting and measuring,* London, Routledge.
5. CLARK, M. R. (1962) 'Ends and means in evaluating the teaching of arithmetic,' *The Slow Learning Child,* **9**, 24–33 and 98–101.
6. FOGELMAN, K. R. (1970) *Piagetian tests for the primary school,* Slough, N.F.E.R.
7. LOVELL, K. (1971) *The growth of understanding in mathematics,* London and New York, Holt, Rinehart & Winston.
8. Nuffield Mathematics Project (1970/73) *Checking up guides I* and *II,* London, Murray and Chambers.
9. Schools Council (1966) *Mathematics in the primary schools,* London, H.M.S.O.
10. Schools Council (1967) *Mathematics for the majority,* London, H.M.S.O.
11. TANSLEY, A. and GULLIFORD, R. (1960) *The education of the slow learning child,* London, Routledge.
12. VERNON, P. (1949) *Manual* for *Graded arithmetic-mathematics test,* London, University of London Press.
13. WEDELL, K. (1973) *Learning and perceptuo-motor disabilities in children,* London, Wiley & Sons.

7. Remedial teaching: some general principles

To have any real chance of resulting in success remedial treatment must have direction and purpose....[7]

It was said in the Introduction that it is not always possible to identify a specific underlying *cause* of a child's learning difficulties; sometimes a child's problems may stem from a combination of several adverse factors. Nor is the precise cause necessarily of crucial importance in planning special help for the child; a remedial teacher has to take the pupil as he is at the time—that is to teach him from the stage he has already reached with his existing experiences, accumulated knowledge and skills. Efficient diagnostic *testing* will have indicated (i) the level the child has reached in the particular skill, (ii) any significant gaps or points of confusion in his knowledge or experience acquired so far, (iii) the next level of instruction to be attempted, and (iv) any significant weaknesses which may need to be remedied or bypassed by avoiding one particular method and selecting a more appropriate one. Diagnostic *teaching* will then take over, and as the teacher observes the child's response to the programme and his rate of progress, the approach will be varied and the materials carefully selected to produce optimum improvement and enhance the child's self-confidence. Careful *record keeping* by the teacher will reflect the outcome of this individualised teaching.

The points above relate quite as much to the child with a specific learning disability (for instance, dyslexia) as to the child with more generalised backwardness. Whether a child's perceptual difficulties, for example, are the result of some subtle dysfunction of the nervous system, lack of neurological maturity or just plain lack of previous experience or teaching, we are still likely to prescribe the same type of training and experience for him. Rates of progress will vary, of course, but teaching strategies remain very much the same.

In recent years there has been increased interest in *differential diagnosis* of children with learning problems. This term means

84

attempting to assess a child's own relative strengths and weaknesses across the range of processes and functions in which he is tested. If a deficiency in any area is particularly apparent it should have an important bearing on the future teaching programme for that child. This approach is typified by such diagnostic instruments as *Illinois test of psycholinguistic abilities* (*ITPA*), the *Frostig test of visual perception,* and certain Reading Readiness Profiles. The results of differential diagnosis have frequently been misunderstood by the time they reach the teaching situation; and at times they result in what almost amounts to a 'spare-part surgery' approach to remediation. Phillips[6] compares the procedure to the systematic tracing of faults in a motor-car to locate the component which requires replacement: and he points out that in human beings, unlike motor-cars, one cannot replace a faulty component. In the differential diagnosis one may find that a child's visual memory for sequences or his ability to pick out a figure from a confusing background are 'faulty' or significantly weak. We cannot replace a unit which will put these matters right; the analogy is false. It may not even be possible or desirable to train separate processes or functions in isolation. Some functions may possibly be improved through training, but not in a way which will then enable the the child to apply them to the learning of a particular skill. For example, to train a child in *visual closure* (the process of mentally or physically completing unfinished shapes or figures and recognising incomplete figures) may do nothing more than make a child better at doing just that, and not improve readiness for reading at all. With some of the commercially produced perceptual training material it is difficult to see how the skill being taught can lead to improved readiness for reading, unless concurrently and by chance it has improved the child's ability to attend to a learning task.

The work of Kirk and Kirk[4] has been abused to some extent by teachers seeking to improve separate abilities in the child by prescribing specific training with little chance of generalisation. Kirk and Kirk, however, make it quite clear that 'Teaching is not discrete but integrative' (p. 121); and, 'It is preferable to develop abilities in a natural everyday situation rather than in an artificial setting, and to train abilities directly in the performance that is required' (p. 130).[4] The point is also made by Wedell who states, '... research evidence strongly indicates that the child needs to learn how to apply his sensory and motor organisation skills to the specific educational task. *Help for failure in basic educational attainments would therefore seem to be best directed to those attainments themselves'* (p. 114— my italics).[8]

The criticism of being over-specific in the training of abilities which are thought to underlie the mastery of basic educational skills relates more to reading and number readiness than to language development programmes where a more generalised approach is inevitable. The same criticism may apply to those forms of training in basic logical processes where it is hoped mental structures will be created which can be used in other 'thinking situations'. The golden rule to remember in remedial teaching is to make any training link as closely as possible with the educational skill you are trying to develop; for instance, in pre-reading activities, if visual discrimination needs to be developed it is more likely to benefit from the use of letter shapes and word shapes than pictures of pigs, ducks, farm gates and kites.

One specific function which is specially worth attempting to improve is the child's *attention span* for a learning task. Many pupils fail to learn because basically they fail to attend.

A few general principles to guide remedial teaching can be gleaned from the field of programmed instructional methods, and these, together with a few additional points below, provide a framework upon which to build remedial programmes. The principles are: (i) to present a learning task by breaking down the stages involved into very *carefully graded steps*; (ii) each step should be simple enough for the child to *succeed* when he makes a response; (iii) the provision of *reward and reinforcement* through not only the feeling of success but from positive *praise and encouragement* (it is sometimes also useful to let the pupil plot his own progress on some form of chart, giving visual evidence of improvement); (iv) situations which require the child to be *actively involved* are more likely to hold the child's *attention* (in some circumstances 'attention holding devices' are useful, such as puppets, card games, pictures, etc.); (v) with slow learners more *repetition* of the units of instruction are required if they are to be assimilated and mastered: teaching should involve *over-learning* (that is, continuing to teach and revise beyond the point at which the child first seems to grasp an idea). Since repetition and over-learning are necessary within the teaching programme for children with learning difficulties these must not be achieved at the expense of enjoyment and motivation—otherwise 'the more we repeat the less we attend'. *Games* provide an opportunity for such repetition with enjoyment; and well-structured games can certainly teach.

It has been suggested that perhaps it is not only helpful to use a certain amount of drill and repetition in the basic teaching of slow learning or disadvantaged children, it may be one of their more efficient learning methods for the mastery of some basic skills.[1234 7] Provided teachers are striving to teach skills with materials which are meaningful and important they should have no fear about using drills to achieve their goal. It is when learning is left to chance that the child with learning difficulties is at risk.

Perhaps the most important ingredient to ensure enjoyment in learning is the teacher's own personality and outlook. A teacher with enthusiasm can make even a flashcard game exciting and enjoyable. In terms of reading progress and improvement no other single factor has greater weight and influence than that of *teacher performance*.[9] All would agree with Tansley's statement that a good relationship between teacher and child is an essential prerequisite to remedial teaching. Lawrence[5] goes much further in suggesting that individual sympathetic counselling of retarded readers can achieve as much as remedial teaching. Certainly a remedial teacher should see it as an essential part of his job to improve the self-image of a child who identifies with *failure*.

Suggestion for further study

Read again the general principles outlined on page 86. Add to this list any other principles which you consider should be taken into account when attempting to teach basic literacy or numeracy skills to slow learners.

References

1. BEREITER, C. and ENGELMANN, S. (1966) *Teaching disadvantaged children in the pre-school*, New Jersey, Prentice-Hall.
2. HIRSHOREN, A. (1969) 'A comparison of the predictive validity of the revised Stanford-Binet and the I.T.P.A.' *Exceptional children*, **35**, 517–21.
3. JENSEN, A. (1970) 'Hierarchical theories of mental ability' in DOCKRELL, W. (ed.) *On intelligence*, London, Methuen.
4. KIRK, S. and KIRK, W. (1971) *Psycholinguistic learning disabilities: diagnosis and remediation*, London and Urbana, University of Chicago Press.

5. LAWRENCE, D. (1973) *Improved reading through counselling*, London, Ward Lock.
6. PHILLIPS, C. J. (1973) 'Specific learning disabilities,' *Remedial education*, **8**, 5–11.
7. TANSLEY, A. E. (1967) *Reading and remedial reading*, London, Routledge.
8. WEDELL, K. (1973) *Learning and perceptuo-motor disabilities in children*, London and New York, John Wiley & Son.
9. WIDLAKE, P. and BELL, L. (1973) *The education of the socially handicapped child*, London, Nelson.

Recommended Reading

McCREESH, J & MAHER, A (1974) *Remedial Education: Objectives and Techniques*, London, Ward Lock.
OTTO, W, McMENEMY, R & SMITH R. (1975) *Corrective and Remedial Teaching* (2nd Ed) Boston, Houghton Mifflin.
WIDLAKE, P. (ed) (1977) *Remedial Education: Programmes and Progress*, Harlow, Longman.

8. Teaching or training readiness skills

Research has found quite clearly that readiness can be trained to a useful extent.[2]

Lack of readiness for learning a particular skill may have been diagnosed as the result of some of the questions/answers on the Infant Observation Schedule (page 6), the Reading Readiness Assessment (pages 46 and 47), or from discovering that the child lacked basic number concepts and was incapable of even the simplest written work using number symbols. A warning has been given that 'lack of readiness' should not spring too rapidly to mind when dealing with children of junior and secondary age ranges, unless the child exhibits obvious perceptual handicaps. The warning is repeated here.

This section outlines briefly some of the activities and some of the available materials which will help to develop readiness for learning, particularly in the skill areas of reading, writing and number. It also lists books which contain details of readiness programmes and activities. The work outlined in this chapter should be viewed as instruction at LEVEL O, corresponding with STAGE O determined by testing (page 46).

Oral language

This is the most important feature of any readiness programme. If a child's oral language development and experience of language fall below a certain minimum level it is unreasonable to expect him to make much progress with reading. Systematic attempts to improve a child's language facility should be built in to all aspects of readiness training.[11] Structured language development programmes are described more fully in Chapter 9, and that section of the book should be read alongside the brief suggestions made here.

Two main points are worth making at this stage:

89

(a) Language should be used to accompany and reinforce the training activities in other sections of the programme. For example, the appropriate words may help to direct a child's perception in a task requiring visual discrimination, giving a word which describes a shape or pattern, talking about the ways in which two pictures differ—even giving the child verbal directions to help in the copying of a shape, 'Up, across, down, round, and down'. The child can then use the language to regulate his own movements.

(b) A more specific aim is to prepare for the vocabulary and sentence patterns which will be met in the early stages of the reading scheme to be introduced later. The names of the characters (Peter, Jane, Cathy, Mark, Janet, John, Mike, Mandy, Roderick, Gregory, etc.), and the important nouns included in the early books (house, trees, toys, etc.). Most good reading schemes have introductory material to make this task easier for the teacher. With the least able children this work will need to be covered more slowly and carefully than with the average and bright children.

The use of the teacher's large Sentence Maker from the *Breakthrough to literacy* material can also help at this stage. To see simple sentences built up using separate word cards can help to bridge the gap between spoken language and language in print.

The sentence structure of early reading books ('Here is a ...', 'This is ...', etc.) can deliberately be introduced informally by printing a child's comments about his or her own paintings or drawings on the actual sheet while the child watches.

Chapter 2 in the book *Aids to reading* by Hughes[4] contains some other useful suggestions which the remedial teacher may wish to use.

Form perception and visual discrimination

If oral language is adequate, and if the child has realised that the marks on paper represent words which can be spoken, the next important skill to consider is that of form perception, which at its highest level is reflected in the fine discrimination of letter sequences.

If a child is very poor at form perception (and this is rare unless he is mentally, physically, and/or perceptually handicapped), the teaching will need to begin with fitting hardboard shapes into inset-formboards, matching and sorting simple regular shapes, and feeling these shapes hidden within a puzzle box where the child can handle but not *see* them. He then identifies the shape just handled from a set of line drawings outside the box. Later the activity can be reintroduced using small-case plastic letters of the alphabet in the puzzle box: these being handled and then identified in the same way. This activity is also useful for holding attention through enjoyment. The catalogues from Educational Supplies Association (ESA), Philip and Tacey, and E. J. Arnold will provide details of form-boards and plastic letters.

Other useful activities, including copying regular shapes using lollie sticks, drawing around templates, drawing within stencils, tracing figures and completing unfinished figures, will also help to develop awareness of shape and form and encourage attention to detail.

The sequence for training visual discrimination should follow the stages:
1. Picture matching→ 2. Shape matching→ 3. Letter-like shape matching → 4. Letter and word matching.

The point at which to begin training will have been indicated by a visual discrimination test (such as Daniels and Diack *Test 4*). The closer the training material comes to using letter and word shapes the more likely it is to be preparing the child for reading.

Some very useful suggestions for worksheets, games and apparatus are included in the books by Hughes[5] and Tansley.[11][12] ESA have a series of booklets for training visual discrimination. The following items from Philip & Tacey will be found useful: *Hereward observation and matching sets, Discrimination picture and shape matching sets, Visual discrimination boards,* and *Letter discrimination inset boards, Letter sorting strip books.*

Visual discrimination exercises can rapidly give way to picture-word matching games, word-to-word matching and simple flashcard work: one is then on the threshold of reading.

Remember, if a child is able to sort and match word shapes and has adequate language development, then he is ready to read through one of the various whole-word approaches.

Visual retention and visual sequential memory

It is helpful for some children to be trained in the careful observation of visual material which they are then required to reproduce from memory in correct sequential order. This is frequently done using picture cards (for example, cow, house, man, cup, ball); but it is more useful if the material used provides letter sequences, for example

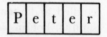

The *Action picture* and *Word making cards* from Philip and Tacey are useful for this work at a simple level.

Sometimes the training requires the child to look at the sequence then, after a short space of time, draw the material or write the sequence of letters.

Hand-eye co-ordination and motor control

The building, cutting, sticking, threading, tracing, jigsaw making, etc., which go on in all infant classrooms are already developing this skill for most children. A few will need much longer at such tasks, and may benefit from specific training.

If the child's balance and general co-ordination are very poor (the Clumsy Child Syndrome) teachers are referred to Kephart's book[7] for suitable activities to include in P.E. lessons. Hughes[6] provides a few suggestions for remedial P.E.

Large-scale chalkboard work using big movements is a useful starting point; and in cases of very poor control it is helpful if the teacher guides the child's hand in order to make the movements smooth and rhythmical, and to establish a correct habit pattern. Simple mazes and dot-to-dot patterns produced as worksheets are found useful by many teachers. Worksheets from the *Frostig programme*[3] (if available) are appropriate here, but the first book from *Early to read*[12] contains useful exercises for hand-eye co-ordination.

Some of the Marion Richardson[9] writing patterns can be used for both chalkboard work and assignment sheets; and the *Training in basic motor skills* workbooks (ESA) complement these very appropriately since both lead to the skills important for handwriting. It is vital that children who do have some degree of difficulty in co-ordination are taught correct letter formation and that handwriting should not be left to incidental learning. Some··books which are useful for teaching handwriting are listed in Appendix 5.

Problems of laterality (that is choice of a particular hand for manual tasks, a particular eye for leading in visual performance and the choice of a particular foot for kicking) and directional sense (grasp of orientation) are frequently found to be present in slow learners and children with specific learning difficulties. These factors are rarely the cause of a child's learning problems but rather another associated symptom. Although some American therapists would claim that unless one first establishes a strong lateral preference in a child other attempts at remediating educational skills are only dealing with peripheral symptoms, most remedial teachers do not deliberately set out to rectify crossed-laterality or to alter hand preferences in their children. Crossed-laterality, lack of firmly established lateral preferences, and poor directional sense frequently result, both in reading and writing (including written number symbols), in a marked tendency to reverse shapes. In extreme cases mirror writing may be produced by the child. It is quite normal for young children up to the age of six-and-a-half to seven years to confuse letters like *b d p* in their reading and writing; and undue attention to this problem would be out of place in the teaching of infants. However, reversal problems which in some cases continue through to secondary school level do require attention. Several ideas for helping children with this difficulty will be found on page 21. Here it is only necessary to stress that if a child is given a correct motor-cue for letter and number symbol formation in the early stages many of the reversal confusions would not persist. Usually giving the correct motor-cue means guiding the child's hand in chalkboard and crayon work. Very useful advice is contained in the manual *A multi-sensory approach to the language arts* by Beth Slingerland (1971, Educators Publishing Service, Cambridge, Massachusetts).

Other sources of visual and visual-motor training activities

Chapter 3 in Tansley's book[11] gives details of a comprehensive perceptual training programme which covers form perception, hand-eye co-ordination, visual copying, visual memory, completion and closure, appreciation of visual rhythm, temporal sequencing, visual discrimination, etc. The programme contains some very useful ideas, but in the case of just one or two of the suggested activities it is difficult to detect a logical progression which leads to the threshold of reading: the transfer of training seems to be assumed rather than proved.

A series of workbooks under the title *Look* have been produced by

Brennan, Jackson, and Reeve (1972, Macmillan). These cover most of the processes listed above.

Training in basic cognitive skills is a series of 28 workbooks by Haskell and Paull (1972, ESA). Skills such as visual discrimination, orientation, sequencing, motor-control, are included in the progression of work.

The flying start kit (D. H. Stott), available in Britain through Holmes McDougall, is an extremely useful set of well-structured games and puzzles. Some of the games the child can complete on his own, some require other players or at least a partner. The group and pair games are designed to train a child to work with others and to await his turn, the demands at each level are reasonably simple and the success rate is, therefore, high. Most of the games are self-checking. Stott[10] claims that the games condition the distractible child to attend, the impulsive child to think things out rather than guess, and the timid child to 'have a go': in other words the materials develop positive learning habits. The puzzles, as well as training (or encouraging) attention, can be seen to involve visual discrimination, picture completion, interpretation of picture material, appreciation of sequential order, and orientation. The learning of simple 'Say and do rhymes' which involve listening and moving also teach a simple vocabulary of prepositions, verbs, adverbs, and adjectives. Other language experiences can be included informally as the games are played. Highly recommended for young slow learners, the kit leads usefully to the first stages of the *Programmed reading kit* (see pages 116 to 120).

The first stage in the *Holt basic reading system* (Holt, Rinehart & Winston) contains 240 instruction units designed to develop auditory discrimination, memory, expressive language, motor control, visual discrimination, visual memory and logical thinking.

Auditory training

It has been shown conclusively that in the process of learning to read auditory skills are just as important as the processes and subskills of visual perception. Progress beyond the stage of building up a basic sight vocabulary using a whole-word approach is dependent upon the development of phonic skills. The acquisition of phonic skill is in turn dependent upon adequate auditory discrimination, auditory analysis, auditory blending, and short-term auditory memory. It is likely that these processes are also involved to some extents in spelling ability.

Auditory training need not always precede any introduction to reading unless a child's auditory perception is markedly deficient; where necessary, auditory training should be provided alongside the child's early reading experience while a basic sight vocabulary is being built up. Many of the activities which are used to teach basic phonic knowledge and word-building skills are also simultaneously training listening skills (for instance, many of the games from Stott's *Programmed reading kit* are developing auditory discrimination, auditory analysis and auditory blending, as well as teaching the sound-symbol relationships involved in the game).

One of the principal aims of auditory training is to increase awareness of sound patterns, to encourage careful attention to speech sounds and to develop the skill of listening. In terms of increasing listening skills in general teachers may find the first unit from *Concept 7–9* (E. J. Arnold) useful, together with some of the *Listening tapes* from the Remedial Supply Company, Wolverhampton.

Two very useful sources for ideas on training early listening skills are: Monroe and Rogers *Foundations for reading* (chapter 4), published by Scott-Foresman (1964); Russell and Russell *Listening aids through the grades*, published by Teacher's College, Columbia University (1959). The books by Hughes[4][5] and Tansley[11] contain useful ideas; and an article by Westwood[14] collects together suggestions from teachers.

Brief consideration will be given to the four auditory processes referred to above:

(a) *Auditory discrimination.* A set of pictures from ESA, *Pictures for sounds,* provides a good starting point. These 26 colourful pictures present opportunities for discussion and for focussing attention upon specific speech sounds. A teacher will also find it helpful to collect pictures from mail-order catalogues and/or a set of the *Pixie miniature* and *Groundwork coloured picture stamps* from Philip and Tacey to use in games requiring the child quickly to touch one of a pair of pictures when a word is called: for example, 'pear' (pear:bear), 'three' (tree:three). Worksheets can also be made with pictures of objects which the child must identify when the initial sound is given. The *Domain phonic workshop* (Oliver & Boyd) contains similar sheets already prepared. When games like these have been played it is useful to get a child to say the name of each picture clearly, and then to listen to his own voice played back on a tape recorder. Even getting a child to repeat aloud word-pairs from a test like Wepman's or Test P5 from the *Domain phonic test* can be of value: for example, 'Say, *could*: *good*'; 'Say, *leg*: *led*'; 'Say, *class*: *glass*' etc. For children in the primary age range the three books in the *Sounds and rhythm* series by Mavis Hampson (Ginn) contain simple little poems and rhymes to practise common speech sounds; they help both listening and articulation in an enjoyable context. Classroom games which involve 'Finding the odd one out' (for example, *b*oy *b*one *b*ag tree *b*and) and which may involve rhyme (for example, s*and* h*and* feet l*and* b*and*) are popular; also, with young children 'I spy' games using initial sounds rather than letter names are useful. Some of the tapes from the Remedial Supply Company and the *Listening to sounds* tapes (E. J. Arnold) should certainly be included in the auditory training programme.

(b) *Auditory analysis*. Some of the above activities have included simple levels of auditory analysis—isolating the initial sound. Games can be extended to listening for final sounds (for example, 'Put a line under the pictures that end like *snake*'. Pictures show r*ake* bucket *cake* ball).Tansley[13] suggests that it is useful to teach sounds as they occur at the end of words since the sound is more strictly phonetic and pure.

Auditory analysis can be taught, or at least encouraged to develop as a skill, by spending a little time in taking words apart into their component sounds; that is, raising the process to the level of awareness in the child. For instance, with a picture of a frog: 'What's this Jackie? Yes. Good. It's a frog. Let's listen to that word frog. Let's say it very slowly. *Fr -o- g*. You try it.' This only involves listening, not reading.

(c) *Auditory blending*. This is also referred to as sound blending or phoneme blending, and is the complementary process to that just described above. Encourage the children to gain experience in putting speech sounds together to build a word—'I spy with my little eye something that looks like a *fr-o-g*'. Use the same technique while reading or telling a story to the children: for example, 'The boy came to the wall. He couldn't get over, and the *d-oor* was *st-u-ck* ....' Children quickly supply the words as the story goes on. Sound blending will also be helped in the early stages of word-building described later.

(d) *Short-term auditory memory*. It is questionable whether this function can be improved with training. Certainly some poor short-term retention is due to lack of *attention,* and any strategies which improve and develop careful listening are likely to influence short-term retention of auditory sequences. Some experts recommend getting the child to repeat sentences (simple messages, for example), deliberately making them a little longer over a period of time. The learning of simple rhymes and jingles may also help. What is necessary is to identify the child with extremely limited immediate memory span so that a different approach is developed for him when word-building skills are taught (see pages 31 and 50). This is one area of weakness which may need to be bypassed through the selection of an alternative teaching approach.

Pre-number experiences

Basic to number work is the concept of *conservation of number,* that is, a group or set composed of N separate items remains a set of that number regardless of how it is arranged or distributed. Lovell[8] has indicated that for five to six year-old children the number of members of a set may appear to alter if the members are rearranged spatially, and experience has to be given to pupils to help them understand conservation of number.

Much of the infant classroom experience of sorting, giving out materials, one-to-one matching, and counting should be helping basic concepts of conservation to develop. For some children the process needs to be made more explicit, and some of the apparatus and materials listed below will help with this.

The *vocabulary* of early number situations and relationships needs to be introduced carefully and systematically to accompany such experiences; and for the least able this vocabulary needs to be repeated and over-learned until totally assimilated (for example, same, different, more, less, many, few, all, none, as many as). Bell[1] provides a list of many of the words contained in a vocabulary of mathematics, and a list is also provided in Appendix 1.

An extremely useful chapter on 'Readiness for mathematics' may be found in Williams,[15] although his advice that arithmetic be delayed until the ESN child is in his ninth or tenth year may be open to misinterpretation and abuse. If the term 'arithmetic' is taken to be synonymous with 'meaningless computation' then few would disagree; but if the 'arithmetic' is a meaningful recording of an operation which the child has just performed with actual materials, then this can be achieved well before nine years of age for most slow learners.

The following activities and apparatus may help a child to develop the concept of conservation of number: teacher-made cards with pictures, dot patterns, sticky shapes and so on can be sorted into groups and sets of equal size (numbers in the sets should be below ten on each card and no number symbols be introduced); matching one-to-one various patterns shown on cards or worksheets; counting activities to establish one-to-one correspondence between the number rhyme 'one, two, three, four' and sets of actual objects, and to establish 'equivalence' or 'difference' between sets or groups to be compared; matching real objects (Airfix soldiers, unit blocks, counters, etc.) to pictures or dot patterns.

Recording, if done at all by the child at this stage, will be in the form of picture representation, not using number symbols.

USEFUL APPARATUS

Croydon number and picture matching tray (Philip & Tacey).

Conservation of number sorting cards (Philip & Tacey).

Conservation structure and pattern making underlay cards for use with *Unifix structural apparatus* (Philip & Tacey).

250 Counting and sorting toys KN883 (E. J. Arnold).

Larne number flashcards KN949 (E. J. Arnold).

Counting and sorting tray N1403 F (Galt).

400 pegboard and 100 pegs (Galt).

100 wooden figures for sorting N1613H (Galt).

Intro-Set I N1413B (Galt).

USEFUL BOOKS

Beginning mathematics, Books I & II. L. Sealey and V. Gibbon (Blackwell).

Mathematics for schools: Level I, Books I & II. H. Fletcher and R. Walker (Addison-Wesley).

Number readiness Books I-IV (Hulton).

Let's explore mathematics Book 1 (to page 27) L. Marsh (Black).

Number rhymes and finger plays E. Boyce and K. Bartlett (Pitman).

Suggestions for further study

(a) Design a graded series of worksheets which will help a child to improve his control over a writing or drawing instrument. Remember that such training should lead to the actual basic skills of letter formation and the correct formation of numerals.

(b) Make a tape-recording which is designed to improve a child's auditory discrimination. Remember that such material is most likely to influence progress in the phonic aspects of reading if speech sounds (phonemes) are used for the training.

Use the tape with a child and note any necessary modifications required.

How would you link the final stages of training in listening skills to the actual teaching of phonics and word-building?

(c) Using pictures cut from mail-order or educational suppliers' catalogues, gummed shapes, dot patterns, line drawings, etc. (see page 98), make a game of at least fifty cards which can be sorted into equal 'sets'. E.g. six ducks, six dots in dice-pattern, six dots in random pattern, six trees, six green triangles, six tally marks; eight pigs, eight dots, etc.

References

1. BELL, P. (1970) *Basic teaching for slow learners*, London, Muller Educational.
2. DOWNING, J. and THACKRAY, D. (1971) *Reading readiness*, London, University of London Press.
3. FROSTIG, M. and HORNE, D. (1966) *Programme for the development of visual perception*, Chicago, Follett Publications (from NFER).
4. HUGHES, J. M. (1970) *Aids to reading*, London, Evans.
5. HUGHES, J. M. (1972) *Phonics and the teaching of reading*, London, Evans.
6. HUGHES, J. M. (1973) *The slow learner in your class*, London, Nelson.
7. KEPHART, N. (1960) *The slow learner in the classroom*, Columbus, Ohio, Merrill Books.
8. LOVELL, K. (1971) *The growth of understanding in mathematics*, London and New York, Holt, Rinehart & Winston.
9. RICHARDSON, M. *Writing and writing patterns*, London, University of London Press.
10. STOTT, D. H. (1971) *Manual for flying start kit*, Guelph, Ontario, Brook Educational (from Holmes McDougall).
11. TANSLEY, A. E. (1967) *Reading and remedial reading*, London, Routledge.
12. TANSLEY, A. E. (1972) *Early to read* (Reading Scheme), Leeds, E. J. Arnold.
13. TANSLEY, A. E. (1972) *Basic reading*, Leeds, E. J. Arnold.
14. WESTWOOD, P. S. (1972) 'Feedback No. 1,' *Remedial Education*, **7**, No. 2, 17–20.
15. WILLIAMS, A. A. (1970) *Basic subjects for slow learners*, London, Methuen.

9. Improving oral language

A child's ability to interpret oral language is vital to future academic success and overall intellectual development.[4]

This section makes one assumption, namely that a teacher has made an effort to identify a group of children within the class who may benefit from regular, systematic, structured attention to their language deficiencies. In some schools there may only be one or two such children; in other areas the background may be generally impoverished, and language development will be a high priority for very many of the children.

The main theme in this chapter is that we do not teach oral language skills as systematically as we attempt to teach reading or number skills; we leave oral language improvement very much to chance, hoping that incidental learning and development will take place. Merely surrounding a child with an enriched language environment is insufficiently positive for the least able: he requires a planned approach with clearly defined objectives quite as much for language improvement as for any other skill.

Most language intervention programmes started in America and have been directed towards improving communication skills among 'minority, disadvantaged groups'. In these programmes language has been the central core of a curriculum which usually includes perceptual training, readiness activities, simple number concepts and problem solving. In general the work has been done with young pre-school children; much less has been attempted with older pupils. Claims are made that 'crash' programmes bring about almost immediate short-term gains in both communication skills and in measured intelligence, sometimes advancing the child's psycholinguistic age by two years in only two months of training. But it is argued that this progress is not maintained after the programme ceases, and that intervention does not 'close the gap' between privileged and under-privileged children. However, the case against language development programmes frequently seems to be overstated; improvements have, in some cases, been maintained for over three years after the programme ceased—intervention cannot be expected to work miracles. Space does not permit a review of the arguments for and against intervention programmes: these may be found in a book edited by Stanley,[7] particularly in the papers therein by Beilin and Bereiter.

Bereiter's main conclusion is that intervention programmes which have a strong 'instructional [that is didactic] emphasis' and are designed to include verbal reasoning, problem solving and the over-learning of language structures achieve far more than informal approaches to pre-school education. The programmes devised by Bereiter and Engelmann[2] are among the best known of those with a heavy instructional bias; and for that very reason are disliked by many teachers in Britain.

It should be borne in mind that American 'minority groups' may be very different from the groups described as 'disadvantaged' in Britain, and their needs may be slightly different. Widlake,[8] for example, considers that the vast majority of young children in Britain will have acquired a grasp of syntactical patterns which will be sufficient for most purposes of communication. However, one has only to observe the struggle which many young E.S.N. and other slow learning children have in understanding teacher language, and more still in framing their own responses, to know that their ability to utilise these patterns is inadequate for the demands of early schooling. There is a need for systematic teaching here.

Before offering a frame-work for language development strategies, it may be useful to consider four ways in which teachers some-times operate to restrict language development, or indeed at times train children *not* to listen.

(i) The teacher uses a language structure (sentence length and complexity) and an expressive vocabulary which the child cannot readily understand and use owing to a lack of previous experience of language at this level of sophistication. This point applies as much at secondary school as it does at infant level. Over a period of time it results in a learned inattention to teacher's voice.

(ii) In the classroom the teacher poses questions which can be answered too readily by a 'yes' or 'no', or by a one-word answer. This does no harm to children already articulate, but equally it does nothing to improve the expressive use of language by the children in need of such opportunity. Mattick[6] writes, 'Do I really listen to children? Or do I jump in with an answer as soon as I think I have guessed what he means ...'—a timely warning. It would, of course, be tedious and inappropriate to expect all answers from pupils to be given in complete sentences; but the ability to construct an answer in sentence form should be something to foster in children who are markedly deficient in language. It is worth setting it as a tangible objective even in work with senior slow learners since improvement is still possible.[5]

(iii) The teacher allows discussion sessions to be dominated by children who are already fluent speakers. It is argued that those who do not actually take much part in the discussion still benefit from hearing what others say, they may pick up new ideas and extend their receptive vocabulary. This may be true at senior level, but there is no evidence to support it at pre-school and infant level. Cazden,[3] looking at some of the language development programmes, comments that a child's communication ability is improved by what *he himself practices saying*, not by what he has the chance to hear.

(iv) There is evidence that, owing to size of class, there are some quiet children who are not forthcoming and with whom a teacher may never converse directly over a period of weeks. Such children will have been spoken *at* (the language of control and direction which is almost inevitable in the handling of large groups) but not talked *with*.

It is, therefore, important to identify the children in need of special help in language development. As far as possible their actual present level of performance will have been evaluated along the lines set out in chapter 3 of this book, and the teacher will have some idea of their immediate needs which she will cater for in the structuring of her programme.

Upon what principles should the language programme be based?

(i) Create an *enjoyable, entertaining, social* learning situation which gives pleasure to the children because they succeed in meeting demands made on them. Again, *teacher personality* is a vital factor.

(ii) Keep the group *small*, not more than five or six children.

(iii) Arrange for *frequent, intensive* sessions, remembering that most of the American programmes are based on two or three short sessions daily.

(iv) Ensure *active participation*, remembering that it is what a child practises saying, not what he hears, that improves communicating ability.

(v) Have clearly defined, short-term *goals* for each session: these may be the teaching and over-learning of certain adjectives (tall: short, thick:thin, tiny:huge), or adverbs (quickly:slowly), or encouraging the linking of two simple statements by the conjunctions 'and' or 'but'.

(vi) Observe the principle that, just as in most situations with slow learners, some degree of *repetition* and *over-learning* is necessary. It is on this line that Widlake[8] is particularly critical, 'Programmes which place great emphasis on reiteration of sentence patterns have the wrong emphasis for British conditions....' The present writer disagrees. If basic language patterns, including such forms as correct plurals and verb tenses, are to become *habit* responses overlearning is necessary.

(vii) Use material such as pictures and games to hold attention and as the basis for language stimulation. The pictures selected for any particular session may provide the opportunity to introduce the specific words to be taught (for example, ' a *tall* green tree', '*short thick trunk,*' '*thin* branches'). Sometimes Matrix pictures can be prepared to teach specific language patterns:

1. *The man* is taking the dog for a walk.
2. *The lady* is taking the dog for a walk.
3. *The boy* is taking the dog for a walk.
4. *The girl* is taking the dog for a walk.
5. (Wow! Am I tired!)

Different picture strips can be prepared to represent different language patterns as illustrated above. The strips can be mounted one above the other on a card and the matrix so formed can be 'read' vertically as well as horizontally. For example, reading

vertically down a column the pictures may show '*A lady is* taking
the dog for walk, ... going shopping, ... painting the door, ...
cutting the grass, ... eating a cake'. Read horizontally, a row
would indicate *a man, a lady, a boy, a girl* performing the stated
action, as in the above example.

(viii) Use *pleasure* and *praise* as reinforcers.

What is the framework upon which the programme should be based?

The aim is to improve functional level in at least two processes,
RECEPTION and EXPRESSION, and is represented diagram-
matically in fig. 2.

Fig. 2

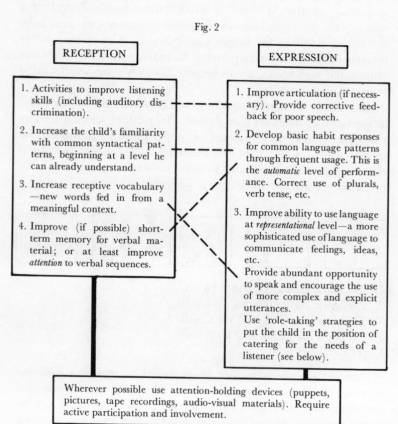

RECEPTION

1. Activities to improve listening skills (including auditory dis-crimination).

2. Increase the child's familiarity with common syntactical pat-terns, beginning at a level he can already understand.

3. Increase receptive vocabulary —new words fed in from a meaningful context.

4. Improve (if possible) short-term memory for verbal ma-terial; or at least improve *attention* to verbal sequences.

EXPRESSION

1. Improve articulation (if necess-ary). Provide corrective feed-back for poor speech.

2. Develop basic habit responses for common language patterns through frequent usage. This is the *automatic* level of perform-ance. Correct use of plurals, verb tense, etc.

3. Improve ability to use language at *representational* level—a more sophisticated use of language to communicate feelings, ideas, etc.

   Provide abundant opportunity to speak and encourage the use of more complex and explicit utterances.

   Use 'role-taking' strategies to put the child in the position of catering for the needs of a listener (see below).

Wherever possible use attention-holding devices (puppets, pictures, tape recordings, audio-visual materials). Require active participation and involvement.

It is clearly not feasible to work within all these dimensions in one session, even though some operate reciprocally (see broken lines of interaction in diagram above). The imaginative teacher will be capable of planning and carrying out language development programmes from this information, but it may also be useful to examine some of the existing kits and programmes already available which are described below.

Teaching materials

(i) *Peabody language development kits* by J. Smith, L. Dunn and K. Horton (produced by the American Guidance Service but available in Britain from N.F.E.R. Test Agency).

This material is designed to stimulate the receptive, associative, and expressive aspects of oral language development and to enhance intellectual and educational progress. Most of the items in the kits are used to attain clearly defined objectives built in to 180 standard lessons. The rationale upon which the Peabody kits are based springs from the hypothesis that cognitive development is facilitated by the mastery of the structure of language.

Level P, which is the most expensive kit and comprises puppets, records, picture posters, picture cards, figurines, magnetic shapes, plastic fruit, etc. covers the mental ages three to five years. *Level I* caters for mental ages four and a half to six and a half years. *Level II* for mental ages six to eight years. *Level III* for mental ages seven and a half to nine and a half years.

(ii) *S.R.A. language programme*, and *S.R.A. listening laboratory* (from Science Research Associates, Henley-on-Thames). The language programme is mainly designed for the six to nine years age range. The programme contains 96 Language Builder Story-boards. Its purpose is to aid the development of receptive and expressive language using eighteen areas of general interest (for example, 'The Family', 'Leisure', 'Workers of our Land'). The listening laboratory, mainly for the seven to eight years level but also found useful for slow learning children in the lower secondary school, comprises taped material, 'Look and listen books', wall chart, answer keys, etc.

(iii) *Pictures and words*, E. Goodacre (Blackie). Designed for the normal five to six years age range, or older slow learners. A fairly simple language development programme linking conveniently with early reading skills. The teacher's manual is particularly useful. The set contains large pictures for discussion work and sets of books for the pupils. All illustrations are in black and white only.

(iv) *Talkmore project* (produced by E. J. Arnold). Mainly for infants and lower juniors with language problems. The aim is to stimulate discussion and foster the development of speaking, listening and early reading skills. The kit comprises wall pictures, concertina books, figurines, flashcards, and Packette tapes. The material has been found useful with immigrant children learning English.

(v) *Concept 7–9* (produced by E. J. Arnold for Schools Council). This can be described as a course in language and reasoning for children in the primary and lower secondary remedial departments.

Unit 1: Listening and Understanding Pre-recorded tapes and work-sheets designed to increase auditory attention and oral/aural comprehension. Responses required of the child are simple, but involve careful listening.

Unit 2: Concept Building Designed to increase the child's skill and flexibility in classifying. Introduces the language of classification.

Unit 3: Communication Designed to increase the child's oral skills of description and enquiry. Particularly useful for the 'role taking' strategies referred to in fig. 2 (page 104); for example, one child may have to describe a strange creature very clearly so that his partner can find the correct illustration. Giving an accurate description makes the speaker consider the needs of the listener. These activities link very usefully with suggestions in the Gahagan book cited below.

(vi) *Language activities kit* (Scott-Foresman Co). Materials and apparatus are suitable for the five to six year-old age range and link with reading readiness activities.

(vii) *The dialect kit* (E. J. Arnold for Schools Council). This material is designed to help the child with West Indian Creole dialect to establish correct forms of plurals, past tenses and subject-verb agreement. Both oral and written work are involved.

(viii) *The language project* (Macmillan).

I *Language in action* Provides attractive and stimulating materials for the development of listening, speaking, reading and writing. Level 0 is termed 'Pre-Literacy'; Level 0–1 is concerned with the alphabet and Levels 1, 2 and 3 with basic language structures. The material includes books, frieze, duplicator master-sheets and resource book.

II *Language guides* These are series of books for the teacher.

At the time of going to press this project is still in course of production.

Source books

The following books all contain ideas for language development:

BEREITER, C. and ENGELMANN, S. (1966) *Teaching disadvantaged children in the pre-school*, New Jersey, Prentice-Hall.

ENGLE, R. (1966) *Language motivating experiences for young children*, Los Angeles, University of Southern California.

GAHAGAN, D. and GAHAGAN, G. (1970) *Talk reform*, London, Routledge.

MEYERS, E., BALL, H. and CRUTCHFIELD, M. (1973) *Kindergarten teacher's handbook* (sections only), Los Angeles, Gramercy Press.

SHIACH, G. McG. (1972) *Teach them to speak*, London, Ward Lock Educational.

The following four books provide ideas for teaching based on the *I.T.P.A.* model:

BELL, P. (1970) *Basic teaching for slow learners*, London, Muller Educational.

KARNES, M. (1968) *Helping the young child develop language skills*, Washington, Council for Exceptional Children.

KIRK, S. and KIRK, W. (1971) *Psycholinguistic learning disabilities: diagnosis and remediation*, University of Illinois Press.

WIDLAKE, P. and BELL, L. (1973) *The education of the socially handicapped child*, London, Nelson.

Readers are also strongly recommended to read Moss, M. (1973) *Deprivation and disadvantage*, Milton Keynes, Open University Press. This book contains sample activities from both the Bereiter and Engelmann programme and Marion Blank's language programme.

Suggestions for further study

(a) Using a large colourful picture as the focus of attention, plan in detail a 15–20 minute language extension lesson with clearly defined aims. Remember the points set out on page 103.

(b) Consider the problems presented by an immigrant child (top infant) with almost no grasp of the English language. How might a teacher attempt to provide some systematic help?

References

1. BELL, P. (1970) *Basic teaching for slow learners*, London, Muller.
2. BEREITER, C. and ENGELMANN, S. (1966) *Teaching disadvantaged children in the pre-school*, New Jersey, Prentice-Hall.
3. CAZDEN, C. (1972) in STANLEY, J. C. (ed.) *Pre-school programmes for the disadvantaged*, London and Baltimore, Johns Hopkins Press.

4. HEBER, R. *et al.* (1972) *Rehabilitation of families at risk for mental retardation*, Madison, University of Wisconsin.
5. McKEOWN, W. D. (1973) *The generalised use of language stimulation and the language-experience approach to reading with older E.S.N. children*, unpublished dissertation, Manchester College of Education.
6. MATTICK, I. (1973) The teacher's role in helping young children develop language competence, *Australian Pre-School Qtly.* **14**, 18–26.
7. STANLEY, J. C. (ed.) (1972) *Pre-school programmes for the disadvantaged*, London and Baltimore, Johns Hopkins Press.
8. WIDLAKE, P. and BELL, L. (1973) *The education of the socially handicapped child*, London, Nelson.

Recommended Reading

MEERS, H. J. (1976) *Helping our children Talk*, Harlow, Longman.

10. The teaching of reading

The normal developmental sequence in the acquisition of reading skills

(i) *Pre-reading experiences.* For most children a carefully structured pre-reading programme is unnecessary: once the child has adjusted to the demands of school life instruction in reading can, and should, begin. For a few it will be valuable to provide pre-reading experiences which prepare the child for beginning reading and take him to the threshold of simple word recognition (see chapter 8). Training in listening skills, encouraging a liking for stories, ensuring familiarity with language patterns, all will form important parts of the programme. When the pre-reading activities involve word-to-word matching, word-to-picture matching, letter and word copying, and the recognition of one or two words from flashcards, the child is entering the next stage of development.

(ii) *Early reading skills.* The first activities will clearly overlap with those just mentioned above; and will usually link with the main reading scheme in use in the school or involve the simple sentence building experiences related to *Breakthrough to literacy.* After preparatory work with flashcards, discussion pictures, sentence cards, the first book in a scheme is soon introduced and/or language-experience books are produced by the children.

Less able children will need much longer at this stage with far more attention given to preparation before the first book is introduced and more over-learning of material. Word recognition games with flashcards, lotto, picture-word dominoes and so on will help to provide revision and reinforcement.

So far the approach will have been almost entirely whole-word (look and say). The sound values of letters will not have been stressed, although many children making good progress will begin to

109

generalise and abstract basic phonic knowledge for themselves. The emphasis will have been upon building up a basic sight vocabulary. Fairly soon, unless the child has auditory perceptual problems, phonic skills should be brought into clearer focus.

(iii) *The development of phonic skills.* The children making good progress will continue to develop insight into symbol-sound relationships and word structure without much specific guidance; but the process is more positive and efficient if the skills are taught. For the less able child or the child with specific reading disability, it is essential that this teaching takes place and learning is not left to chance. A sequence for the teaching of phonics is suggested on page 113. The teaching of single letter sounds, digraphs and blends should be carried out partly using the words already known by sight ('a' for 'astronaut', 'Bl' for 'Blackpool') and partly from phonic games and blackboard work. The blackboard work will also stress word-building skills—how to sound out letters, how to recognise and use groups of letters—in order to tackle new words.

It has been found that lack of systematic instruction in phonics and the absence of an organised teaching programme are apt to characterise the schools which are least successful in the teaching of reading.[3][10]

(iv) *The development of higher order reading skills.* At this stage the reader is making much greater use of context to aid 'skilled guessing' in word recognition. Performance is swift and fluent. There is a complete understanding of what is read, leading to increased enjoyment in reading and the ability to read for information. There is the development of independent study skills, the ability to read and abstract information and detail, to increase vocabulary, to scan for important features and to utilise reading as a tool in all other subject areas.

The basic needs of the backward reader

Most of the needs of the backward reader are dealt with in detail in the instructional levels (pages 114–125); the list below merely forms a summary:

(i) An improved self-image through counselling, 'success' situations, praise and encouragement, recognition of own progress.

(ii) A teacher who is sympathetic and enthusiastic.

(iii) Specific training in certain sub-skills for just a few children.

(iv) Auditory training prior to the introduction of phonics for some children.

(v) Longer spent on early flashcard work and sentence building.

(vi) More time spent in over-learning and mastery of material before the next level of instruction is attempted.

(vii) Careful preparation before each new book is introduced so that the stories are read at success level rather than frustration level.

(viii) Systematic teaching of phonic knowledge and word-building skills.

(ix) A carefully graded programme, which may mean the making of extra supplementary material (worksheets, card games, etc.) to use alongside a scheme to make the programme match the child and not vice versa.

(x) The need for correct letter formation and handwriting teaching as part of the programme.

(xi) Finger-tracing and other multi-sensory approaches may be needed to aid auditory-visual integration and assimilation for a few children.

(xii) If child-produced books are used, either alongside a scheme or instead of the early stages, it must be in a highly structured manner in order to teach reading.

The use of reading schemes

It has become popular to be ultra-critical of reading schemes, because control which has to be exercised over vocabulary and sentence structure and the need for adequate repetition of words and phrases in the early books result in rather stilted language and a poor story line.[12 16] It is considered that this is best avoided, and language-experience materials are proposed as a suitable alternative. In many cases, however, the criticisms of reading schemes reflect adult rather than child reactions. Reading schemes have not been superseded, and are likely to continue to be an important part of the total reading programme; they provide a system and framework which might otherwise be lacking from the teacher's approach. Just as it is totally wrong to view a reading programme as merely 'working through the books of a scheme and hearing children read as often as possible', so it is equally wrong, particularly for the least able, to think that one can do without a scheme.

In selecting a scheme teachers should consider the following features:

(i) *Attractive format.* This is particularly important when selecting material for the older backward reader. The books should contain illustrations which are attractive and in keeping with the interest and maturity level of the pupils who will use them.

(ii) *Vocabulary control.* This should be indicated in the Teacher's Manual and/or recorded in the back of each book in the series. Some knowledge of the new words to be introduced in a book will allow the teacher to prepare the way for that story. In general, many schemes are too steeply graded for the least able pupils, particularly if supplementary readers, workbooks, and apparatus are not used alongside the main books.

(iii) *Supplementary materials and books.* Consideration should be given to the amount of supplementary material available within a scheme, remembering that a teacher who does not use the material provided is at once removing much of the structure from the scheme and cannot, therefore, complain if it fails to teach some children to read.

As far as possible some of the supplementary materials should involve writing activities as well as reading.

A scheme which lacks supplementary material may still be useful provided the teacher makes suitable worksheets, games and so on for use with the slow learners.

(iv) *Length of book.* It is important that the early books in a scheme should be fairly short. Nothing recedes like success if a child is on the same book for many weeks.

(v) *Ratio of print to illustrations.* Illustrations provide useful cues in early reading; early reading books should contain many pictures and the amount of print on each page should be correspondingly less. The number of illustrations will be reduced as the books increase in difficulty; but publishers should avoid presenting large masses of print for children who are poor readers.

(vi) *Size of print and sentence length.* The size of print is important in the early stages of learning to read, whether the learner is a child or a non-literate adult. Large print reduces the need for fine visual discrimination; and single lines of print reduce figure-ground confusion (that is they prevent visual distraction from surrounding letters and words). It is particularly useful in early books to try to present one viable unit of information—a meaningful phrase or short sentence—per line; in intermediate and higher level books the sentence complexity should not be too far removed from the children's own expressive speech patterns. Over-complex language can greatly reduce readability of the material even when the child can 'read' the words.

(vii) *Attention to phonics.* Some schemes do not claim to cater for instruction in phonics, leaving the teacher to introduce it when appropriate, while such teaching forms the main emphasis in others. When dealing with children who are not making normal reading progress such schemes are particularly useful—even if a teacher's main scheme is very much biassed towards a whole-word approach, a second-string scheme used alongside could provide the extra attention to phonics and word-building for those who need it. Such support is available from *Royal road readers* (Chatto & Windus), *Step up and read* (University of London Press), *The look out gang* (Gibson), *Sound sense* (E. J. Arnold), and *Teenage twelve* (Gibson). (See also recommended schemes and supplementaries in Appendix 6.)

(viii) *Interchangeability with other schemes.* Most teachers find it useful to introduce some variety into the reading material by using books from several different schemes or sets. How they fit together is usually determined by some fairly subjective assessment of the material in the books which are then allocated to certain grade levels. It can also be done through the use of a readability formula or readability chart, references for which can be found in Appendix 5 (c). A useful cross-reference system for a wide selection of books is provided by Moon.[9]

Suggested order for dealing with phonic skills

As far as possible all phonic instruction should make use of words already known to the child by sight. Any phonic principles studied should be reinforced by the provision of carefully prepared material which embodies the words in a meaningful context.

Stage 1 Teach the common single letter sounds (vowel and consonant), introducing each one as the initial sound in words already recognised by the child ('c' and 'g' should be given their hard sound).

Stage 2 Stress the common short vowel sounds as embodied in simple words: e.g. hat pet pin log hut.

Stage 3 Simple word-building and sound-blending based on the material from Stages 1 and 2.

Stage 4 Teach common digraphs and blends *ch sh th st bl tr*.

Stage 5 Simple word-building and blending from stages 1, 2, 3, and 4.

Stage 6 Teach vowel digraphs *oo ee*.

Stage 7 Teach, over a period of time, *gr cr br cl pl wh ck* etc.

Stage 8 Word-building and phonic dictation using material from all stages above.

Stage 9 Modification of first vowel by a final *e* (mad: made, etc.).

Stage 10 Word analysis and synthesis to consolidate all the above stages. Stress common syllable units.

Stage 11 Extra work on endings, if necessary, *s es ing er ent*.

Stage 12 Vowel digraphs *ai ay ea oi oy ie oa ou au*.

Stage 13 A consideration of some of the 'exceptions to the rules'. Particular attention to spelling.

Levels of instruction for children with reading difficulties

These levels of instruction relate to the Stages of Development outlined in chapter 4.

LEVEL O

This has been covered in the Readiness Training section pages 89–97.

LEVEL 1

The individual is ready for reading and may already recognise a few words by sight.

(i) *Increase basic sight vocabulary.* Work will continue with flashcards, picture-word matching, word lotto games, etc., using commercially produced apparatus or materials made by the teacher. *Basic word lotto games* (Galt), *Word lotto* (Remedial Supply Company), *Ladybird key-word games* (Wills & Hepworth) will be found useful at this stage. Important sight words or phrases can also be prepared for use with the *Language-master machine* (Bell & Howell) which allows a flashcard to be displayed visually at the same time as the child can hear the word pronounced or can record his own voice on to a tape strip attached to the card. It is very useful indeed for self-help and revision of words taught in other situations.

For the senior non-literate individual greater attention may be focussed upon a basic sight vocabulary of words necessary for social competence (such as *danger, poison, keep out, pay here*). A set of cards, suitably authentic in appearance, is available from Philip & Tacey (*Essential notices flashcards*).

At this stage the *Sentence maker* from the *Breakthrough to literacy* material (Longman) can be used, or the *Colet sentence building cards* (Philip & Tacey).

Whenever and wherever possible the visual work on word recognition should be reinforced through writing activities.

If the child has great difficulty in remembering the material being taught it is vital to limit the amount of new work introduced in any session. It is extremely valuable for some children, particularly those with severe reading disability, to use a multi-sensory approach to help with the assimilation and retention of a few sight words or a few single letter sounds. This approach usually requires the child to finger-trace over a word which has been written by the teacher in blackboard-sized writing on a card, while the child, together with the teacher, pronounces the word slowly and clearly as he traces the letters with his finger. If the child already knows his letter sounds he may, if the word is phonemically regular, sound out the letters rather than articulate the word. This is repeated several times until the child thinks he can write the word correctly from memory. When he is successful at this, he writes the word into his language-experience story and/or enters it into his spelling dictionary. The word cards are kept by the teacher (ideally in an index box) and used for frequent revision. This approach, although time consuming and arduous, does bring results and is of maximum value to the child who has problems of integration (combining the visual impression of a word with its auditory-vocal equivalent). Multi-sensory approaches are also referred to as V-A-K (visual-auditory-kinaesthetic) or V-A-K-T, with 'T' implying that tactile sensation is also stimulated through the use of textured letters cut from embossed wallpaper or made from sprinkling fine sand over the word written with a 'glue-stick'. Tactile sensation is rarely required in ordinary school remedial situations, but a much greater use of V-A-K could help many slow learners to assimilate and retain early reading material. For a more detailed coverage of multi-sensory approaches teachers are referred to Fernald,[5] Cotterell,[4] Blau,[2] and Wolff[19]—the application of such approaches to reversal problems is dealt with later in this chapter.

In general, the teaching at LEVEL 1 will be mainly through a whole-word approach; but it will be useful to begin work on letter sound values and very simple word-building with any child who does not require pre-phonics auditory training. If auditory training is required see pages 94–7.

(ii) *Developing basic phonic knowledge.* As far as possible phonic instruction should begin by making use of words already known to the child by sight. In addition, and to provide more systematic teaching, the following materials will be found helpful: the first five games from Stott's *Programmed reading kit*, using all three colour families in the correct sequence; the introductory books from the *Royal road reading scheme*; the following items from Philip & Tacey: *Sort and sound cards, Action pictures and word matching, Approach picture and word building cards, Colet alphabet-picture matching cards*; from Galt, *The phonic self-teacher* and *Initial sound and picture matching cards*. For the teacher wishing to make her own materials, for example sets of pictures to match against the correct letter symbol, the *Pixie miniature gummed stamps*, and the *Groundwork gummed stamps* (both from Philip & Tacey) will prove invaluable.

The early stages of the *Clifton audio-visual reading programme* (E.S.A.) may be introduced for the senior pupil or adult illiterate provided the individual is keen to learn. This stage in the programme covers basic phonics and simple word-building.

The *Pictogram system* devised by Lynn Wendon could be adopted for the primary school child who may enjoy an imaginative story and would be helped to remember the sound values of letters and letter blends by such an approach. The material is organised at two levels and may be purchased from Pictogram Supplies, Barton, Cambridge.

Another attractive and entertaining medium which helps primary children to remember letter sounds and to succeed with word-building is *Reading by rainbow* by E. and W. Bleasdale (Moor Platt Press, Bolton). This approach uses a simple colour coding system involving only four colours to enable the irregularities in our spelling to be bypassed to some extent. For example, silent letters are coloured pale yellow and are ignored; black letters give their common *sound*; red letters give their *names*; blue is used for the long 'oo' sound and to indicate the letter *d* to avoid confusion with *b*. There are six books in the set, a reference card, worksheets and teacher's notes.

(iii) *A structured use of the language-experience approach.* One method which provides an opportunity to combine both whole-word and phonic approaches is the language-experience approach. At the same time, the method allows the individual to move away from a reading scheme with which he associates failure and to make progress through using reading material based on his own interests and language patterns.[18] This approach is particularly suitable for the older child or adult who is a non-reader.

Oral language rather than the printed page is the starting point. The central theme within the language-experience approach is epitomised in the statement, 'What I think about I can talk about. What I say I can write or someone can help me to write down. What I write I can read'.[1] It is a flexible approach which can be adapted to meet individual needs and can include any specific remedial teaching considered necessary from the results of diagnostic testing.

The stages involved in using the approach in a highly structured way are summarised below and should not be viewed as separate lessons. It is impossible to predict in advance how long a child will need to spend in gaining mastery of the material at each stage; it may require only one session, or it may need to be spread over several.

Stage 1 As a result of some recent experience or current interest (such as a visit to a local factory, a t.v. programme just seen, a favourite speedway team), the teacher discusses the topic with the child using appropriate language to structure the situation. From this discussion a simple sentence which the child wants to write must emerge. The teacher may need to influence the actual choice of words so as to include several that occur early in the basic sight vocabulary list (McNally and Murray).

Example We went to the old lighthouse

The teacher writes the sentence for the child; both read it together and the child then 'reads' it unaided. Although the child may merely be repeating it from memory rather than reading that does not matter at this stage. The child then copies the sentence into his language-experience book (or if he has very poor motor control, traces over the teacher's writing), and then adds an illustration while the teacher is attending to other pupils. If an old type-writer is available in the classroom the child can then type out the sentence for use in the next session.

Stage 2 This should follow as soon as possible after *Stage 1*, ideally later the same day while using the method in its early stages.

The child tries to read back the sentence from the previous session, with help if necessary. The sentence is also written or typed on a strip of paper or card which the child cuts up to form separate word cards. The child takes the cards and tries to arrange them back in correct sequence to form the original sentence. This can only be done by careful attention to the characteristics of the individual words. If he cannot rearrange the cards correctly he is allowed to look back to the original in his book and match the words against it. He continues to practise until he can succeed with the task.

The word cards are now used by the teacher as miniature flashcards to train word recognition out of context of the sentence. The teacher makes a note of any persistent errors and the child files the cards away in an index box, word bank or envelope attached to the inside cover of his book. Some teachers find it useful to affix two envelopes inside the cover of the book, one to contain the words which are mastered by the child, the other for words which the child does not know or confuses; these are then used in future sessions for revision and over-learning.

Stage 3 Revise previous material using sentence or sentences in book and word cards.

New sentence material is introduced and used as suggested in *Stages 1* and *2* above.

This work may continue for several pages of the child's book over a period of instruction lasting, say, four or five weeks. The sentences used may reflect various new interests and experiences or, with the older person, may continue along one theme. Words which are definitely known by the child without hesitation can be entered on a chart in the back of the book to provide visual evidence of progress. A copy of the McNally and Murray *Basic sight vocabulary list* forms an ideal check list for this purpose; the list is glued to the inside cover of the book and words are underlined in coloured ink when known by the child. The teacher can see at a glance, for instance, that although ten pages of work have been produced three early key-words have not yet been used. This can then be put right in the following sessions.

Stage 4 Unless there is a good reason (such as auditory perceptual problems) to avoid doing so, a start can now be made on teaching basic phonic knowledge from the initial letters of words already known by sight: *l*ighthouse, *l*ike, *l*orry, *l*ady, *l*ittle, etc. This stage needs to be supplemented with work from Stott's *Programmed reading kit* and some blackboard work to extend the experience with phonics. The list on page 113 should provide some guidance. A little later other phonic-sight habits can be developed from the language-experience material. For example, a twelve and a half year-old boy writing about the making of a footstool in handicraft lessons introduces the words *chisel* and *drill*. This provides the opportunity to teach other words beginning with the *ch* digraph (*ch*op, *ch*at, *ch*alk, *ch*eese) and *dr* (*dr*op, *dr*ag, *dr*y, *dr*ess).

Once this stage is reached phonic dictation should be used to reinforce the learning of words which have just been studied, getting the child to write them from memory.

Stage 5 When it seems that the child has developed adequate reading ability from his own language-experience books the introduction of a reading scheme or set of supplementary readers can be anticipated. To ensure that the child succeeds when the first book is introduced the teacher can determine the new words which he will need to know and teach them by means of word recognition games, word study and, if possible, using them in the written work in the language-experience book.

Once a reading scheme is in use the language-experience approach becomes the child's free writing activity and the word index box or word list can serve a useful purpose as a self-help spelling list.

Some final points. (a) If a particular child has difficulty with learning and retaining the basic sight words or the sound values of certain letters in phonics, it may be necessary to use the V-A-K technique described on page 115. (b) At some stage a child will almost certainly need to practise the sight words being taught and put right points of confusion. This is the time to use games like word lotto or board games involving frequent reading and/or spelling of the words. (c) For the child with poor auditory perception the method described above will still be useful since it can be modified to delay any introduction to phonics until a later stage. Auditory training can be provided while the child is still using a predominantly whole-word method. (d) Handwriting will need to be taught as a skill in order to make the recording of language-experience material a fairly simple task. (e) The theme, topic or centre of interest must change before the individual tires of it. (f) The teacher must keep adequate records of work covered, otherwise the structure and system will vanish from the approach and little real progress will be made; if used inefficiently this approach becomes nothing more than the making of scrap-books. Frequent revision, over-learning and careful teacher-control of material are the vital factors to ensure success.

Teachers who may wish to explore the more general uses of the language-experience approach are referred to Stauffer[15] and Rodwell.[12]

Teachers using *Breakthrough to literacy*, which is commercially produced language-experience material, are advised to consider the stages described above in connection with the least able children in their classes. Are they imposing sufficient structure and control— providing enough over-learning?

LEVEL 2

If the language-experience approach has been followed through as outlined above it will have overlapped LEVEL 2 to a considerable extent. On the other hand, if it has not been used at all we are now dealing with a child who has made some progress in reading, largely through a whole-word method. Phonic skills require development.

In addition to the materials suggested below, a child will benefit at this stage of development from some of the educational television programmes designed to improve reading (e.g. B.B.C. *Look and read*).

(i) *Basic sight vocabulary*. There may still be gaps to be filled in the child's sight vocabulary; diagnostic testing will have revealed precise needs. The word lotto games will still be useful, and for older pupils the game *Wordmaster major* (Macdonald Educational) will prove enjoyable and beneficial. Teacher-made word lotto games may be designed to cover special needs, such as a tendency to ignore word endings and to guess from the initial letter; the lotto game would use words all beginning with the same letter or letters and only differing in final letters (*his, hit, him, hill, hid*).

(ii) *Phonic knowledge and word building*. This will be the main emphasis at LEVEL 2 and Stott's *Programmed reading kit* will become increasingly useful. Games 1 to 5, teaching the basic single letter sounds and a few digraphs may still be needed by some, also the games 'Half-moons' and 'Brickwall I' for word-building, and 'Port-holes' and 'Which of two' for phonic-sight habits. For some simple word-building and spelling the *Word maker* from *Breakthrough to literacy* can be introduced here.

Word-slides, word-wheels and word-building card games are beginning to become very useful at this level. The following books contain detailed suggestions for making such material: Moyle (ch. 11),[11] Hughes (ch. 5),[6] Webster (ch. 8),[17] Jackson.[7]

Other appropriate materials:

Vowel and digraph word completion slides (Philip & Tacey)

Phonogram workbooks (4 in set) (Philip & Tacey)

Phonic practice cards (Galt)

Some of the *S.R.A. word games* used selectively (S.R.A.)

Word study units for the *Language master* (Bell & Howell)

Tapes from the Remedial Supply Company

Listening to sounds tapes (E. J. Arnold)

Sections from *Clifton audio-visual reading programme* (E.S.A.)

Early sections from *English colour code programme* (Senlac)

The *Word control sheets* and the *Remedial reading scheme* for use with the
  Stillitron Aid (Stillit Books)

'*I spy*' and '*Pair it*' (Rupert Hart Davies)

Happy words game (Macdonald Educational).

In chapters 7 and 8 of his book Miles[8] suggests a programme which can be commenced at LEVEL 2 and will extend to higher levels of instruction.

(iii) *Reversal problems.* If a child has reached this stage and still confuses *b d p* or *u n*, it is essential that he should be given a motor cue (kinaesthetic training) to establish the correct direction of these letters. Finger-tracing just one of the letters until mastered is probably the most positive way to overcome the problem: first the child should close his eyes (or wear a blindfold) while the teacher guides the index finger of his left or right hand (as appropriate) over the shape of the letter 'b' written on the blackboard; the letter is simultaneously sounded or named as the tracing is repeated several times; the teacher now takes the child's finger over a series of other small-case letters and the child must indicate quickly and clearly every time a letter *b* is traced. This is all performed with eyes closed or with a blindfold; the advantages of this 'modality blocking' are dealt with by Blau.[2] The aim here is basically to give the child a physical image against which to discriminate *d* and *p*. As soon as the

child has mastered one of the letters thoroughly the *Post boxes* game
from Stott's *Kit* can be used, together with a self-help card showing
that 'little b' is really only the bottom half of capital B. This card
can be left on display in the classroom for some time after training.
(iv) *Comprehension.* A tentative start may be made on Ward Lock
Reading workshop 6–10 or the appropriate S.R.A. *Reading laboratory.*
SRA *Lab.1a* has a main interest age range of six to seven years
but covers reading ages six plus to eight and a half years; *Lab.1b*
has a general interest age range of seven to eight years with a reading
age range of six and a half to nine and a half years; SRA *Lab.1c*
has an interest age range of eight to nine years but covers six and a
half to ten and a half years reading age.

LEVEL 3

Reading ability should be increasing well, but phonic skills are still
not fully operational.

(i) *Basic sight vocabulary.* Any gaps which still exist in basic sight
vocabulary must be filled through specific teaching. Flashcards may
also be used to improve spelling of irregular words.

(ii) *Phonic skills.* Much of the apparatus suggested in LEVEL 1 above
may still be needed by some children who are making slow progress
in the acquisition of phonic skills. In addition, the following items
key in at this level: from Stott's *Programmed reading kit*, the 'Brickwall
II', some of the 'Snake games' and 'Find the letter strip II'. The
English colour code programme (Senlac) will become even more useful
at this level, as will sections of the *Clifton audio-visual programme*
(E.S.A.). The *Remedial refresher cards* (Gibson) will provide opportunity for written work, and *Phonic sets*, *Phonic pairs*, *Family pairs* and
Match it (all card games) help with word-building and the develop-
ment of phonic sight habits (all from Rupert Hart Davis). The
Debden suffix changing cards (Philip & Tacey) also aid word-building.

Greater emphasis should be placed upon the studying of word
families, followed by phonic dictation. Very useful at this level will
be teacher-made tapes based on word families, which should aim to
develop insight into word-structure and to teach certain important
phonic-sight habits: e.g. *ail* t-*ail*, s-*ail*, r-*ail*. f-*ail*, p-*ail*, m-*ail*, sn-*ail*,
tr-*ail*. Some work will be done at the blackboard, the children
experimenting with new sounds added to a common unit such as *ail*

or *ight*. The learning sequence will be: study, revise, remember, write from dictation.

For those who have access to, and a liking for, audio-visual equipment the *Talking page* (Ricoh Synchrofax from E. J. Arnold) is most suitable for presenting teacher-made phonic worksheets.

The following books will be found useful as sources for material to be used for word-study sessions; most contain word groups arranged according to phonemic relationship.

General. Some very useful ideas and principles in Appendices 1 and 2 of the Teacher's Manual from *Breakthrough to literacy* (Longman) and in the Manual for the *Data reading scheme* (Schofield & Sims). Appendices 2 and 3 in *The assessment and teaching of dyslexic children* (ICAA) contain lists of sounds and a summary of spelling rules.

Word study material. The Phonic Group tables at the end of the main reading books in the *Beacon reading scheme* (Ginn) are invaluable.

The Word Building books from *Let's learn to read* (Blackie)

Sounds and words (Set of 6 books) (University of London Press)

Sounds of words (Gibson)

Word games Books 1–6 (Gibson)

Sounding and blending (Gibson)

My first, second and *third book of word families* (Philip & Tacey)

The booster workbooks (Heinemann)

Six phonic workbooks (Ginn)

Sound sense (E. J. Arnold)

Basic reading (E. J. Arnold)

Fowler's *Scientific spelling books 1–4* (Holmes McDougall)

Remember, only use word study activities as an extra dimension to the reading programme; over-used they can result in loss of interest.

(iii) *Comprehension.* This is certainly the stage to introduce Ward Lock *Reading workshop 6–10* if not already in use. The S.R.A. *Reading laboratory* at the appropriate level is a very suitable alternative; *Lab.1c* has an interest age range of eight to nine years with a reading age spread of six and a half to ten and a half years. *International lab.2a* covers the interest age nine to ten years and reading ages seven to twelve years.

The teacher may also find it useful to prepare 'cloze' material for the children to use: narrative matter omitting words which the child must supply using his understanding of the context.

Some of the suggestions given in the next level may also be helpful.

LEVEL 4

Since this level is very much concerned with filling gaps or correcting misunderstandings in phonic skill and knowledge, the accurate diagnosis of specific difficulties is essential.

(i) *Consdolidation of word skills.* Having determined the necessary teaching points (see pages 56–7), select appropriate materials from the following sources to teach as necessary:

English colour code programme (Senlac)

Remedial refresher cards (Gibson)

Stott's *Programmed reading kit,* especially 'Brickwalls II', 'Snake games' and 'Long word jigsaws'

Spellaway books 1 and *2* (Schofield & Sims), which will also be useful at LEVEL 5.

The booster workbooks (Heinemann)

Sound sense (E. J. Arnold) used very selectively.

The programme outlined in the book by Miles[8] may provide a suitable framework for some teachers to follow, and chapter 5 in the extremely useful book by Roswell and Natchez[14] should be read alongside it.

(ii) *Improving comprehension, vocabulary and independent word study.* Ward Lock *Reading workshop 9–13*

S.R.A. *Reading Laboratories, Lab.2a.* Interest age range nine to ten and reading age range seven to twelve years.

Lab 2b. Interest age ten to eleven, reading age range seven and a half to thirteen years.

It is not unusual to find that a child with an adequate mechanical reading ability as assessed, for example, by the Accuracy Scale of Neale's *Analysis of reading ability*, does not score so highly when questioned about the content of what he has read. Sometimes his rate of reading is so slow that the child loses the meaning of what he is struggling to decode; others 'read' far too rapidly for them to take in meaning and select important information. A child may also fail to understand fully what he is reading because the words are not in his receptive vocabulary.

The following suggestions may help to improve comprehension: (a) select the most interesting and stimulating material possible at an appropriate level of readability; (b) set, or read through, comprehension questions before the story or passage is read, then the child knows what to watch for and report; (c) give the child experience in retelling a story or passage after he has read it; (d) check that the vocabulary load is not too great and, if necessary, deal with unfamiliar words before the child meets them in print; (e) try to select reading material which links with the child's own interests; (f) make frequent use of 'instruction sheets' which the child must read, interpret, and act upon—for example, carry out a simple experiment, follow a recipe, or make a model; (g) let the child set comprehension questions for others to answer; (h) if the child can cope with it, set assignments requiring the use of reference books.

(iii) *Spelling.* Specific advice on spelling is provided in the next chapter.

LEVEL 5

At this level the individual is functionally literate. Ensure an abundant supply of interesting material at correct readability level; at secondary school level in particular it is important to liaise with the school librarian to make sure that suitable books are readily available in the school library. See Appendix 6 for list of books for Reluctant Readers.

The S.R.A. *Reading laboratories* and Ward Lock *Reading workshops 9–13* both include reading rate builders to develop rapid but careful reading habits. In developing project or topic assignment sheets ensure that the material helps to utilise the skill of reading for meaning.

Suggestions for further study

(a) Take as a starting point any reading scheme or set of books to be used by your least able readers. Design and make a board-game for use with up to four children which will help them to meet, revise, and over-learn the set of new words which they are likely to encounter in each book.

Play the game with a group and consider necessary modifications.

(b) What do you understand by the term 'phonic sight habits'? How might these be developed in a backward reader?

(c) How would you use 'phonic dictation' as an aid to the development of word building and spelling skills?

(d) If a child is considered to be reading at *frustration* level if he is failing to read correctly 30% or more of the words in his book, discover within your own class how many pupils *are* attempting to read at frustration level. What are the implications?

References

1. ALLEN, VAN R. and HALVORSEN, G. (1961) *The language experience approach to reading instruction, Contributions in Reading 27*, New York, Ginn & Co.
2. BLAU, H. and BLAU, H. (1968) 'Some multisensory approaches for the severely disabled reader,' *Reading*, **2**, 5–10.
3. CANE, B. and SMITHERS, J. (1971) *The roots of reading*, Slough, N.F.E.R.
4. COTTERELL, G. (1970) 'The auditory-kinaesthetic technique,' in FRANKLIN, A. (ed.) *The assessement and teaching of dyslexic children*, London, ICAA.
5. FERNALD, G. (1943) *Remedial techniques in basic school subjects*, New York, McGraw-Hill.
6. HUGHES, J. M. (1972) *Phonics and the teaching of reading*, London, Evans.
7. JACKSON, S. (1971) *Get reading right*, Glasgow, Gibson.
8. MILES, T. R. (1970) *On helping the dyslexic child*, London, Methuen.
9. MOON, C. (1973) *Individualised reading*, Centre for the Teaching of Reading, University of Reading.
10. MORRIS, J. (1966) *Standards and progress in reading*, Slough, N.F.E.R.
11. MOYLE, D. (1968) *The teaching of reading*, London, Ward Lock.
12. Plowden Report (1967) *Children and their primary schools, Vol. I*, London, HMSO.
13. RODWELL, E. W. (1972) 'The do-and-say, say-and-write approach,' *Reading*, **6**, 25–30.
11. ROSWELL, F. and NATCHEZ, G. (1971) *Reading disability* (2nd Ed.), London and New York, Basic Books Inc.
15. STAUFFER, R. G. (1970) *The language experience approach*, New York, Harper & Row.
16. THOMPSON, B. (1970) *Learning to read*, London, Sidgwick & Jackson.
17. WEBSTER, J. (1965) *Practical reading*, London, Evans.
18. WESTWOOD, P. S. (1972) 'The language experience approach in the remediation of reading difficulties,' in SOUTHGATE, V. (ed.) *Literacy at all levels*, London, Ward Lock.
19. WOLFF, A. (1970) 'The Gillingham-Stillman programme,' in FRANKLIN, A. (ed.) *The assessment and teaching of dyslexic children*, London, ICAA.

Recommended books on the teaching of reading (in addition to those cited above):

General interest

DIACK, H. (1960) *Reading and the psychology of perception*, Nottingham, Skinner.
FRIES, C. (1963) *Linguistics and reading*, New York, Holt, Rinehart & Winston.

MERRITT, J. (ed.) (1972) *The reading curriculum*, London, University of London Press.

MORRIS, R. (1963) *Success and failure in learning to read*, London, Oldbourne; (1973) Harmondsworth, Penguin.

RAVENETTE, T. (1968) *Dimensions of reading difficulties*, Oxford, Pergamon.

SMITH, F. (1973) *Psycholinguistics and reading*, London and New York, Holt, Rinehart & Winston.

VERNON, M. D. (1971) *Reading and its difficulties*, Cambridge, Cambridge University Press.

Teaching methods and techniques

ABELWHITE, R. (1967) *The slow reader*, London, Heinemann.

BOND, G. and TINKER, M. (1967) *Reading difficulties: their diagnosis and correction*, New York, Appleton, Century Crofts.

DELLA-PIANA, G. M. (1968) *Reading: diagnosis and prescription*, London and New York, Holt Rinehart & Winston.

DURKIN, D. (1962) *Phonics and the teaching of reading*, New York, Teachers' College, University of Columbia.

GATES, A. (1947) *The improvement of reading*, New York, Macmillan.

HARRIS, A. J. (1956) *How to increase reading ability* (4th Edn.), New York, Longman Green.

HEILMAN, A. W. (1968) *Phonics in proper perspective* (2nd Edn.), Columbus, Ohio, Merrill.

KENNEDY, E. C. (1971) *Classroom approaches to remedial reading*, Illinois, Peacock.

MONROE, M. (1932) *Children who cannot read*, Chicago, University of Chicago Press.

MOXON, C. A. (1962) *A remedial reading method*, London, Methuen.

Reading Resources Catalogue, from Centre for the Teaching of Reading, University of Reading.

RUSSELL, D. H. (1961) *Children learn to read*, New York, Ginn & Co.

STAUFFER, R. (1969) *Teaching reading as a thinking process*, London and New York, Harper & Row.

Specialist interest

CRITCHLEY, M. (1970) *The dyslexic child*, London, Heinemann.

CROSBY, R. and LISTER, R. (1969) *Reading and the dyslexic child*, London, Souvenir Press.

KEDNEY, R. and MACFARLANE, T. (1973) *Working with non-literate adults*, Department of Adult Studies, Newton-le-Willows College of Further Education, Lancs.

MEREDITH, P. (1972) *Dyslexia and the individual*, London, Hamish Hamilton.

NAIDOO, S. (1972) *Specific dyslexia*, London, Pitman.

ROBERTS, R. (1973) *Teaching adult illiterates*, Manchester & Salford Council of Social Services, Gaddum House, Queen Street, Manchester.

11. Written work and spelling

Writing, like the early stages of reading, develops most successfully as a record of what is done and known, enjoyed and felt.[2]

This chapter should be read in close conjunction with chapter 5.

Written language

The flow-diagram below (fig. 3) summarises the stages through which the normal child passes in acquiring the ability to use written language for personal recording and communication purposes.

The division between *Creative* and *Utilitarian* aspects of written language is, of course, artificial. Some teachers would argue that simple recording from another subject area, such as mathematics or history, is 'creative' if the child has used his own words and expressed his own thoughts. However, the diagram may help to indicate that it is important to consider just how far the least able pupils may be reasonably expected to proceed down the branch headed *Creative Aspects*. It may well be that there is a definite limit within this channel in terms of the child's ability and future needs as an adult. If it is feasible to restrict the amount of time spent with the least able children in pursuing activities down the creative channel, it may well allow greater time to develop vital skills in the *Utilitarian* channel. Nevertheless, 'it would be equally wrong to confine their writing activities to the sort of composition they might expect to use when they have left school: writing letters of application, making simple factual reports, filling up forms, and so on.'[7]

It is considered that the 'basic minimum for social competence' in terms of writing skill would embrace the ability to write correctly (i) own name(s) (ii) own address (iii) own date of birth (iv) own age (v) own nationality. To this list should be added, if possible, the ability to write a simple letter and send a greetings card, to leave a written message for a visiting tradesman, neighbour, workmate or boss, to fill in at least part of an application form and know where to go for help with the rest.

128

Fig. 3 The development of written language

Primitive stage Child's early drawings and paintings 'tell a story', a fact which is quickly revealed when the child describes them orally.

First writing Usually a copy of the child's own name.

(It is still relevant to ask 'Can he spell his name correctly?' even at upper secondary level. If he cannot do so, priorities have got a little muddled in previous teaching.)

Early copy writing Recording 'news' from the blackboard, etc.

At this stage correct letter formation should be taught.

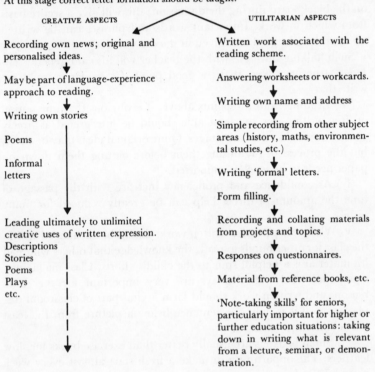

CREATIVE ASPECTS

Recording own news; original and personalised ideas.

↓

May be part of language-experience approach to reading.

↓

Writing own stories

Poems

Informal letters

Leading ultimately to unlimited creative uses of written expression.
Descriptions
Stories
Poems
Plays
etc.

UTILITARIAN ASPECTS

Written work associated with the reading scheme.

↓

Answering worksheets or workcards.

↓

Writing own name and address

↓

Simple recording from other subject areas (history, maths, environmental studies, etc.)

↓

Writing 'formal' letters.

↓

Form filling.

↓

Recording and collating materials from projects and topics.

↓

Responses on questionnaires.

↓

Material from reference books, etc.

↓

'Note-taking skills' for seniors, particularly important for higher or further education situations: taking down in writing what is relevant from a lecture, seminar, or demonstration.

The following general points may be helpful:

(i) Most of the written work should evolve from discussion and experience, the feeding-in and receiving back of new words and phrases associated with the topic or theme. 'The good teacher begins at this starting point, encouraging them to express their views orally and helping them, by questioning, by making suggestions and by the interest and respect he shows for their views, to explore their own potential for thinking about the subjects which have been raised and for expressing their thinking with sensitivity and accuracy. The kind of discussion that many teachers manage to induce in their classrooms is a stimulus to good writing as well as an educative experience in its own right'.[8]

(ii) The slow learner will need to talk through the ideas very carefully, and even revise the sequence of points before putting pen to paper. A very simple outline of the main points may be put up on the blackboard during the discussion; this will give a secure basis from which to work. Important words and phrases can be written up to add to the guidance given in the early stages.

Such 'talking through' with the teacher will also aid general sentence structure: 'Yes, that's a good point, Craig. How could we write that?'

(iii) Leading from the points above, it is obvious that our notion of 'free writing' for the least able should be interpreted as 'freely guided writing' in the early stages. Quite original ideas may be there, but the process of organising them before getting them down on paper needs to be teacher-supported.

(iv) As confidence and proficiency increase with the passage of time the amount of direct help can be greatly reduced for many pupils.

(v) Whenever possible, written work, should be exchanged within the class for other pupils to read; the knowledge that others will read his material is a helpful spur to the child's efforts. Class magazines, newspapers and wall displays are very important for the same reason; and written work should form a vital part of classroom display, even if it is only one sentence below a picture from the least able children.

(vi) Small booklets are usually better than exercise books for slow learners. The opportunity to make a fresh start almost every week is far better than being faced with the accumulation of evidence of past failures which can accrue in an exercise book. For older pupils and adults with literacy problems a loose-leaf file is better than an exercise book.

(vii) It should be a golden rule that no child is expected to fill pages with work he is incapable of reading and has copied from the blackboard. This happens fairly frequently in the subject-specialisation atmosphere of the secondary school.

(viii) Do not be over strict in the marking of written work from slow learners; if the work appears to need a large amount of correction it must either have constituted an original effort on the child's part, and should be accepted as such, or the teacher failed to give enough guidance in terms of talking through the material beforehand, providing word lists and so on to ensure reasonable success. Prevention of mistakes is better than attempted cure, and it pays to anticipate writing needs.

(ix) Train the children to make a habit of 'proof reading' their written work; they will be capable of detecting and self-correcting many errors if they are encouraged to do so.

(x) The frequent use of exercises on punctuation, on 'there and their', on 'too, two, to' seems of doubtful value; the learning (if any) does not readily transfer to a child's free writing. It is much better to teach these points from a child's own work. He will, for example, immediately appreciate where full-stops are needed if he reads his material aloud to the teacher or the class.

(xi) Do not demand too much written work from a less able child unless he wishes to produce a lot. Ensure that what is written is meaningful to the child and comprehensible to others. Standards should be set (and maintained) according to the individual's level of ability.

(xii) Some suitable topics for booklet writing are: *A book about myself,* with personal data—where I live, my family, my friends, what I like, things I hate, etc.; *A book about the people in my class,* with descriptions, opinions, interests, hobbies, interviews, etc.; *A book about this school,* interviews with teachers, caretaker and kitchen staff, plans and measurements, the playground, lessons, etc.; *A book about the district,* linked with environmental studies; *Our visit to* ... ; *My book of horror stories; My book of jokes; My favourite tv programmes.*

Although workcards are available for written work (for example, *Ladybird series* from Wills & Hepworth) most teachers find it useful to make their own card material, using colourful pictures from magazines, colour supplements, art prints and so on suited to the interest level of the pupils. Such cards could have on the reverse side lists of words which the child writer might wish to use in making up a story or description from the picture.

The following books may be found useful by the teacher:

BURGESS, T. *et al.* (1973) *Understanding children writing,* Harmondsworth, Penguin.

CLEGG, A. (1964) *The excitement of writing,* London, Chatto & Windus.

HOLBROOK, D. (1964) *English for the rejected*, Cambridge, Cambridge University Press.

HOLBROOK, D. (1967) *Children's writing*, Cambridge, Cambridge University Press.

MAYBURY, B. (1967) *Creative writing for juniors*, London, Batsford.

PYM, D. and SOUTHWELL, L. (1956) *Free writing* (Bristol University Publication No 10.), London, University of London Press.

These sets of books also contain relevant material:

EYRE, W. (1964) *Imagine and write*, Blackwell, Oxford.

HOLBROOK, D. (1966) *I've got to use words*, Cambridge, Cambridge University Press.

KEE, G. (1972) *The write around cards*, London, Blackie.

LANE, S. M. and KEMP, M. (1968) *Towards creative writing*, London, Blackie.

RALPH, W. (1967) *Creative writing for secondary schools*, London, Edward Arnold.

For younger children:

MILBURN, C. (1972) *Read, write and remember*, London, Blackie.

MILBURN, C. (1972) *Write what you know*, London, Blackie.

Spelling

Remedial help with spelling will vary according to individual weaknesses, but three general principles should be considered:

(i) The pupil must be interested in his own progress and must feel that he is improving.

(ii) The aim of the teaching sessions should be to develop useful 'word study techniques' in the child: the habit of careful looking. From these techniques it is hoped he will be able generally to understand word structure and grasp that sequences of letters occur frequently together to represent units within words. Though many words are learned incidentally, proficiency will be improved if habits of word-study are taught.

(iii) With very weak spellers appeal must be made to as many senses as possible. A word must be seen, listened to and pronounced correctly for the sound characteristics, and written for the 'feel' of it. For some children the colour-coding of certain important cues can be helpful.

Games or puzzles which are enjoyable and provide repetition without boredom are useful, particularly when they reveal answers immediately together with the opportunity for self-correction.

The following activities and exercises may be useful for general or particular use:

(a) One of the easiest aids to make and use is, of course, the flashcard. These are particularly helpful for teaching irregular words, and for the child with poor auditory discrimination or imagery who needs to use a predominantly visual approach. The words are introduced to the pupil on cards about 12" × 4", the word is pronounced clearly and particular characteristics stressed; after about five seconds' exposure the child writes the 'word pattern' from memory, that is, he tries to recreate the image of the word. That 'imagery' can be improved in a way that aids spelling performance is supported by the research of Radaker.[6] The word is not considered to be mastered until the child can write it correctly from memory several days later, and many repetitions may be needed for any one word. For very weak spellers the word may need to be traced several times first.

(b) Use can be made of 'gapped words', with the number and position of the gaps varied according to the complexity of the word. A list of tricky words for revision can be written on the blackboard with certain key letters missing but with the essential pattern of the word still obvious; if the word has a special point of difficulty just that spot can be left out:

e.g. begi*nn*ing sincer*e*ly rec*ei*ve Wed--sday Feb--ary
Some remedial workbooks present words with the letters muddled and the request that the child discover what the word is and write it correctly. It is doubtful if this teaches spelling; it is the kind of task which the good spellers can perform and poor spellers cannot. One important aspect of word recognition is that the characteristic sequence of letters should be seen and recalled; to muddle the sequence would seem to increase the difficulty.

(c) Exercises in which the pupil is required to divide words into syllables or to construct words from given syllables can help. Such activities can be produced as work sheets, with or without a tape-recorded commentary. The 'Long-word jigsaws' from Stott's *Kit* are useful here.

(d) Studying words in 'word families' for reading improvement can be extended to word-study for spelling improvement. As soon as a group of words has been studied they should be reinforced through phonic dictation by the teacher.

(e) The use of word games can be both encouraging and helpful.

Most toy shops sell games such as *Scrabble, Spellmaster, Phonic rummy, Shake-words* and *Lexicon.*

(f) The use of simple graded crossword puzzles can assist word study, and is very useful with the older child.

(g) The importance of treating spelling and speech at the same time cannot be over-emphasised. Words should always be spoken when written, in some cases using a tape recorder to test the child's ability to say the words correctly. He should hear his own pronunciation from the tape.

(h) The action of writing is an essential part of acquiring familiarity with a word pattern. Writing a word several times from copy need not be looked upon as pointless, particularly if the pupil is then asked to write the word again from memory and tested a day or two later. Peters[4] recommends that a child asking the teacher for a word to use in a story should be asked to look at the word carefully once the teacher has written it, then cover it or turn the page and immediately write it from memory before entering it in the story. This is far more positive and systematic than blindly copying the word from the teacher's entry in his word-book.

(i) The use of programmed assignments for use with a linear teaching machine (e.g. *Bingley tutor* from E. J. Arnold; *Autobates machine* from Autobates of Nuneaton; *ESA tutor* from E.S.A.) can be very helpful for individualised teaching. Spelling is one skill which lends itself very well to the principles of programming. A tape recording should always provide the auditory cues in spelling programmes, and the *Talking page* (E. J. Arnold) is also very suitable for the presentation of spelling assignments together with a sound commentary. The use of headphones or an earpiece allows the programme to be used within the classroom without distracting the children not engaged in the work.

(j) A final note concerning the least able pupils: the best time to begin a systematic approach to spelling is when simple 'look-and-say' methods of teaching reading are giving way to the teaching of phonics and simple word-building.

It is pointless to expect a good standard of spelling if a child's reading attainment is very poor. Reading improvement must always precede any attack on spelling deficiencies, although some specific remedial techniques (such as Fernald's) will teach spelling and word recognition simultaneously. It is best to increase attention to spelling when the pupil has achieved a reasonable basic sight vocabulary and some phonic knowledge.

In most classrooms it is useful to compile a core list of common spellings frequently needed by most children in their writing. A copy of such a list can then be available to a pupil when he is ready to develop a self-help approach to his spelling problems.

Some useful books :

ARVIDSON, G. L. (1969) *Learning to spell,* and *Alphabetical spelling lists 1 and 2,* Wellington, New Zealand Council for Ed. Research.

BENNETT, D. M. (1967) *New methods and materials in spelling,* Australian Council for Educational Research.

BURROUGHS, F. (1957) *Vocabulary of young children,* Edinburgh, Oliver & Boyd.

EDWARDS, R. and GIBBON, V. (1964) *Words your children use,* London, Burke Publishing Co.

EDWARDS, S. (1968) *Spelling difficulties step by step,* London, English Universities Press.

FOWLER, W. (1966) *Scientific spelling Books 1–4.* Edinburgh, Holmes McDougall.

FREYBERG, P. (1960) *Teaching spelling to juniors,* London and N.Y., Macmillan.

FREYBERG, P. (1972) *First spelling dictionary,* London, Macmillan.

HILDRETH, G. (1955) *Teaching spelling,* New York, Holt, Rinehart & Winston.

LEECH, D. C. (1958) *A guide to spelling for secondary schools,* London, Blackie.

MIDDLETON, R. (1967) *Senior spelling,* London, Methuen.

SCHONELL, F. J. (1932) *The essential spelling list,* London, Macmillan.

A useful coverage of written work and spelling is provided by Bell (Ch. 6 and 7),[1] Tansley & Gulliford (Ch.7),[9] Williams (Ch. 7 and 8).[10]

Handwriting

Several points concerning handwriting have already been made in chapter 5. Poor handwriting may stem from poor co-ordination, but more usually it is symptomatic of inadequate instruction in letter formation. Regular practice in handwriting is not out of place, even at secondary level; such practice may involve work from the blackboard, from specially prepared worksheets, or from fair copies of stories or letters already written in rough. Correct grasp of the writing instrument, correct sitting position, correct orientation of paper, the production of rhythmic and smooth movements all need to be checked. If, after reasonable remedial help, a child appears incapable of producing legible cursive handwriting he should be encouraged to use script writing only.[3] Even if he leaves school still writing in this form his efforts will at least be legible to others. It should be noted that less able older pupils get a great deal of satisfaction from typing their own work provided that the assignments are fairly short.

Appendix 5 contains a list of books covering the teaching of handwriting. Two articles by Presland[5] are recommended reading. The problems of the left-handed child are dealt with by M. M. Clarke in *Lefthandedness* (1957) and *Teaching lefthanded children* (1974), both published by University of London Press.

Suggestions for further study

(a) Discuss with other teachers their views on the importance which should be placed upon imaginative writing with slow learners. What are your own opinions?

(b) If you are concerned about the standard of handwriting in your class try to bring about some improvement by regularly and systematically teaching this skill. After a reasonable period of time evaluate the results of this drive.

(c) Over a period of two weeks make a note of the words which are most frequently written incorrectly by children in your class. Is it possible to teach the spelling of these words so that they are mastered and give no further difficulty? If not, why?

References

1. BELL, P. (1970) *Basic teaching for slow learners,* London, Muller.
2. Department of Education and Science (1964) *Slow learners at school, (Pamphlet 46),* London, HMSO.
3. GOLDSTEIN, H. and SEIGLE, D. M. (1955) *A curriculum guide for teachers of the educable mentally handicapped,* Danville, Illinois, Interstate Publications.
4. PETERS, M. (1970) 'The teaching of spelling, *Remedial Education,* **5**, No. 2, 76–9.
5. PRESLAND, J. L. (1971) 'A psychologist's approach to backwardness in handwriting' *Remedial Education,* **6**, Nos. 1 & 2 (two articles).

6. RADAKER, L. D. (1963) 'The effect of visual imagery upon spelling performance', *Jnl. Educational Research,* **56**, 370–2.
7. Scottish Education Department (1970) *English for the young school leaver* (Bulletin 3), Edinburgh, H.M.S.O.
8. Scottish Education Department (1971) *English in the secondary school: later stages* (Bulletin 4), Edinburgh, H.M.S.O.
9. TANSLEY, A. E. and GULLIFORD, R. (1960) *The education of the slow learning child,* London, Routledge.
10. WILLIAMS, A. A. (1970) *Basic subjects for slow learners,* London, Methuen.

12. Guiding development in number work

Few subjects appear to cause more uncertainty and misgivings amongst those of us responsible for the education of the less able child than the teaching of arithmetic.[12]

Several writers have pointed out that remedial teachers tend to be ill at ease with the teaching of mathematics and number skills since not only has content changed dramatically but so, too, have methods. It is certainly wise to ask if contemporary approaches to the learning of mathematics are ideally suited to the needs, abilities and learning strategies of the least able children. It may well be that they are—given a competent teacher who is able to provide the correct balance between (for the want of better terms) 'discovery methods' and a more 'didactic' approach. The supremacy of one method over the other has yet to be proved, and most teachers actually arrange the lessons so that 'discoveries' are guided.[24]

The central notion running through the *Nuffield mathematics project* is that 'the children must be set free to make their own discoveries and think for themselves and so achieve understanding, instead of learning mysterious drills'.[9] Fletcher wisely remarks, 'After discovery, you must give the child plenty of practice and time to develop and consolidate his understanding of mathematical concepts. It does not follow that children always remember what they discover.'[5]

The flow-diagram which accompanies Fletcher's excellent mathematics scheme indicates the importance of *real situations, active involvement in learning, language* and *discussion,* and *practice.* Provided that the teacher places more emphasis upon the practice element for the least able and guides more directly their discoveries and the general application of them to other problems, optimum learning with real understanding should take place. Of course, the rate of development will be slower. It should be remembered that concept growth is likely to start later and take longer with slow learners, that abstract mathematical relationships are likely to be beyond their understanding, and that they will be poor at generalising from single experiences or from skills taught in isolation (hence the importance of not teaching drill divorced from previous meaningful experience).

In the past few years several very useful books have been written containing sections dealing with the teaching of mathematics to the least able children. Readers are referred to these authors for a much fuller coverage than is provided here: Abelwhite,[1] Bell (ch.8),[3] Hughes (ch.6),[6] Irving,[7] Tansley and Gulliford (ch.8)[10] and Williams (Ch. 9 to 12).[13]

The following sections are linked directly with the stages of diagnostic assessment set out in Chapter 6. In attempting to keep them concise they inevitably appear narrow.

Following the administration of a suitable arithmetic/mathematics test as PHASE I, the teacher will select appropriately from the other possible PHASES below.

PHASE II

Child's performance very poor.

(i) *Vocabulary.* Fletcher said that one must not allow a child's mathematical progress to be held up by lack of ability to verbalise; but the almost total inability to verbalise found in some children can be a major obstacle which must be overcome. If the child's understanding of the vocabulary associated with number and mathematics is very restricted, greater attention must be given to teaching and overlearning the appropriate terms in a meaningful context. It is not just the vocabulary itself which is important but the syntactical patterns which accompany the verbalisations. For example, '*Are there more* dogs *than* cats? *How many more* cars *than* buses?

(ii) *Conservation of number.* This was dealt with on page 97 of the section on readiness activities. The important objective is to establish in the child a real understanding of the constancy of a set of objects.

(iii/iv) *Sorting and Classifying* (by one attribute, two attributes, etc.). The following apparatus will be found useful: from Metric-Aids Ltd —*Logic blocks* (mx 7019), *Logic diagrams* (mx 7037), *Introsets* (mx-7012), *Grouping sets* (mx 7008); from Philip & Tacey—*Interchangeable plastic attribute elements* (N437), *Table-top logical elements* (N451), *Venn diagram circles* (N457); from Galt—*Attribute blocks* (N1672H); from E. J. Arnold—*Alo-blocks* (SD847); from E.S.A.—*Dienes logiblocs.*

(v) *One-to-one matching* (to achieve equal sets). Any sorting apparatus is suitable for this. It is also important to establish one-to-one correspondence between tally marks or dots on paper and actual objects counted.

(vi) *Counting*. Obviously, if this basic skill is deficient it can only be taught and improved by working with the child individually. Where confusion may arise, if at all, is when counting objects over twelve in number; sometimes the number-word sequence is muddled (fifteen, seventeen, eighteen, etc.), or the child fails to make correct one-to-one correspondence between the word spoken and the objects touched in order. If the physical act of counting a set of objects appears difficult for the child it may be worth examining visual perception in some depth.

(vii/viii) *Recognition of number symbols and correct sequencing of number symbols*. The cardinal value of a number symbol should, of course, be related to a variety of sets of different objects containing that number of items. Teachers can make symbol-to-group matching games (the number 11 on a card to be matched with 11 birds, 11 kites, 11 cars, 11 dots, 11 tally marks, etc.). Useful apparatus: from Philip & Tacey—*New Colet figure-value cards* (N39–1 and N39–2), *Random value and figure matching cards* (N156), *Croydon number and picture matching tray* (N43); from Galt—*Number me* (NO449E).

Also useful are teacher-made number lotto cards containing a selection of the number symbols being taught or over-learned (1 to 10, or 10 to 20, or 25 to 50, etc.). When the teacher holds up a flashcard with the number and calls it the child covers the number on his card. He is the winner if he can later read all the numbers back to the teacher from his completed card. Later these same lotto cards can be used for addition and subtraction games, the numbers on the cards now representing correct answers to some simple statement made by the teacher ('Eyes down for a full house! 5 and 4 make ...? The number 1 less than 8?' etc.).

Unifix structural apparatus (Philip & Tacey), the use of the *Value boats*, the *Inset pattern boards*, the *Number indicators*, the *Value cards*, the *Tens and Unit cards* and the *Notation cards* all teach the recognition of number symbols in a meaningful way. The *Pattern boards*, the *Counting board* and the *Number track* in the Stern Apparatus (E.S.A) serve the same purpose.

(ix) *Writing number symbols*. This should be taught parallel to the above activities. Correct symbol formation should be taught as thoroughly as correct letter formation in handwriting; this will reduce the incidence of reversals of figures in written recording.

There is a danger that a slow learning child will be expected to deal with symbolic number too early. Pictorial recording, dot patterns, tally marks are very acceptable forms of representation for the young or very backward child. Gradually, the writing of number symbols will accompany such picture-type recording, and then finally replace it; by which time the cardinal values of the symbols are really understood. 'Mathematical symbols refer to activities. No one can make sense out of the symbols unless he has carried out actions with materials'.[8]

(x) *Arranging objects in order of size.* This should obviously be taught using concrete materials. Most structural apparatus lends itself to the construction of 'stairs', 'towers', or 'skyscrapers'. Counting forwards and backwards can also be linked with such activities.

(xi) *Ordinal value.* It may be necessary to teach ordinal values like 'fifth' using objects arranged in order (soldiers, cars, a strip-picture of houses. a staircase, etc.). The child should also be able to point out the 'tenth' house in a row without re-counting if he has just correctly identified the 'eighth'.

(xii) *Simple addition and subtraction.* This should emerge as meaningful recording of operations which have just been performed with objects. The acquisition of facility in mental addition and subtraction should not be an end in itself; but when a child fully understands what number bonds represent it is certainly helpful to have these established as 'habit responses'. The danger is in attempting to teach these in isolation and too early.

Partitioning of sets, putting together unequal sets, as well as the recording of the operations involved, help to make number bonds meaningful. Dice games, ring-quoits with scores, simple card games, all help to practice quick addition and subtraction. Dice can be made with other than the 1 to 6 dots on the faces. The *Mathematical games* folio from Macmillan contains some very useful material of this kind.

(xiii) *Counting on.* Counting on and counting back can be taught as useful skills using Number Ladders, Number Tracks, Number Squares, etc. Some teachers argue that children begin to count on and count back when their own level of conceptual development allows this to emerge spontaneously; it is a more positive step (with the least able) to teach this operation.

(xiv) *Recognition of coins.* This can be taught using real money (for some of the time) and facsimile coins and notes. Money lotto and other games help to reinforce learning. Useful apparatus: from Galt: *Fill a purse* (N1843B); *Decimal coin recognition* (N1530C); *Facsimile coins* (N1597A). From Philip & Tacey: *Decimal-aid coinage chart* (N360); *Decimal-aid money value recognition cards* (N358); *Decimal-aid value matching cards* (N483).

In general at this first stage of development the following materials will be found very useful: *Lift off*—a series of six sets of workcards by Bell, Connelly, Ratcliffe (Davis & Moughton); The early stages of *Mathematics for schools, level I* Books 1–7, plus *Teacher's resource book* (Addison-Wesley); *Beginning mathematics* by Sealey & Gibbon (Blackwell); also for the younger children some of the Mollie Clarke: *Number books* from Wheaton.

Teachers will find the Nuffield Guides *I do and I understand, Mathematics begins* and *Pictorial representation* very valuable background reading. For those using structural apparatus the following books are important: *Unifix: Teacher's Manual* by Nixie Taverner and *Group work with Unifix materials* (Philip & Tacey); *Stern apparatus: children discover arithmetic* by C. Stern (Harrap); the following booklets by W. H. Pleuger supplied by E.S.A.: *Number with your children, A guide to the use of the Stern apparatus, Discovering arithmetic.*

Phase III

(i/ii) *Addition and subtraction.* Use partitioning of various sets (counters, sticks) and recording the operations. (For example, a set of 14 can be partitioned to show 7 and 7; 8 and 6; 10 and 4, etc. Follow this with worksheets with examples such as $14 = 7 + \square$; $6 + \square = 14$; $14 - 6 = \square$; $14 - \square = 6$ etc.) Addition and subtraction can also be developed through structural apparatus—Stern's *Number cases, Ten tray, Twenty tray* and *Number track; Unifix Number square* and *Operational board.* Games such as *Quick tens, Quick teens, Domi-numbers, Adding bonds* and *Taking bonds* (Galt) give practice with enjoyment.

Although there is every reason to try to improve a child's speed in performing simple addition and subtraction, the giving of a regular 'mental arithmetic test' on a class basis is hardly the best way to do this; such a procedure only proves to the child that he is not very good, ... it does not actually teach him anything. A more useful method is to provide the child with all the necessary materials to help him to work out the correct answer (counters, number squares, etc.) and allow enough time for him to do this. Each day he will see how many he can get done in, say, three minutes, and will attempt to improve on his own record. The numbers are kept realistically small until he becomes proficient at that level. 'Sum Cards' are essential, but must only form a part of the programme.

(iii) *Written forms of computation.* Once a child has evolved his own forms of recording in the early stages (pictures, dots, tally marks, mapping arrows) there is no reason why conventional forms of both vertical and horizontal computation should not be established. The horizontal form has much to commend it (see PHASE IV below).

(iv/v/vi) *Commutative law, Additive composition, Complementary nature of + and −.* A full understanding of these principles will evolve and will be made apparent to the child in the partitioning of sets, the grouping of sets and the recording of these operations. Blackboard work and prepared worksheets will help to establish the relationship through practice to the point of mastery.

(vii/viii) *The translation of an operation into a recording, and vice versa.* The child should be able to watch as a bundle of ten sticks and two extra ones are added to a set already containing a bundle of ten sticks and three extra ones and then write the operation as $12 + 13 = 25$; or to see four 'tens' rods from the Stern material put with one 'tens' rods and a 'six' rod and write this as $40 + 16 = 56$. The reverse is to show the child a recording in number form and get him to *show* what it means.

(ix) *Translating problems into number terms for solution.* This, of course, is an on-going activity throughout much of the school week: the attendance figures for the day, the number staying to school lunch, the cost of the visit to the seaside, the finances from the school dance can all be used as examples. Much useful work can also come from pictorial representation and charts produced by the class—how many homes have colour t.v.? How many children come to school by bus? How many miles did the coach travel in taking us to school camp (using mileometer readings)? For those who can read it is valuable to use problem cards.

(x) *Recognising larger number symbols and writing larger numbers from dictation.* The use of number tracks, number ladders, number squares and card games all help to establish recognition. There may still be a lag between correctly reading a number and being able to write the number when it is dictated (for instance, 17 may be read correctly as seventeen but written as 71 from dictation owing to the sound of the word; or forty-seven may be written as 407).[14] More frequently, the errors occur with H. T. U. when these begin to be beyond the child's experience—100407 written for 'one hundred and forty-seven'. The implications are obvious; keep the numbers within the realms of reality and make sure that children who need it do get practice in writing them from memory.

(xi) *Telling the time.* The need to be able to tell the time ranks high on the list of important skills for social competence. Children should be taught to tell the time as soon as they are able to recognise numerals up to twelve and capable of grasping the idea of 'minutes past' and 'minutes to'.

It must be noted that 'reading the dial' can be taught as a specific (and very important) skill, whereas appreciation of the passage of time—how long it takes to walk to school, how long it is to lunch time, how long sixty seconds take to pass—can only come from direct experience raised to the level of awareness through discussion.

Apparatus for teaching aspects of Time may be found in the catalogues of Galt, Philip & Tacey, Metric-Aids, etc.

(xii) *Days of the week/Months of the year.* If the child does not know these then teach them rather than expect him to pick them up eventually. Simple work with a class calendar is also very important.

Phase IV

(i) *Reading and writing numbers to 100 and to 1000.* The points made in section (v) above are relevant here also.

(ii) *Finding a number 'three more' or 'five more than', etc.* Where this ability is poor give direct help and practice in precisely this process. It may be necessary to prove what happens when 4 is added to 98 to make 102, (so that it does not make 'ninety-twelve' or 912). Stern's *Dual board* and *Number track* and any form of number square will help to make this operation obvious if a child is still confused. Assignment sheets can be made to reinforce such learning, for example, 'Add 7 to each of the numbers in this list. Check your answer each time using the number track. $74 + 7$; $64 + 7$; $34 + 7$'.

(iii) *Place value.* A misunderstanding of notation and place value is one of the most common problems exhibited by slow learners up to and including those at secondary school level. Frequently the problem has arisen because abstract numbers much too large to be meaningful have been introduced too early.

Place value is made apparent to a child using Stern's *Dual board*, the Unifix *Tens and units trays* and any form of abacus; also, any activity which requires a child to bundle or group sets of ten. This type of experience and this stage of understanding is so important that it should not be taken too hastily; and the recordings of operations must be fully understood. The notational aspects of place value are nicely illustrated for the child by the change in digits observed on any 'click counter' or on the mileometer of a car; the child can see the 9 in the units column give way to a zero while the new ten clicks up in the next position.

(iv/v) *Place value and methods of addition and subtraction*. Much rote learning has taken place in the past to establish correct responses for 'carrying tens', 'one under the line', or in the case of subtraction either 'Borrow ten and make that one less' or 'give the top line a ten and the bottom line a ten'. Abelwhite[1] presents some provocatively horrifying examples of the lack of understanding which accompanies such rule of thumb learning. More recently, the increased interest in providing children with experience in manipulating sets has extended to more meaningful ways of teaching both addition and subtraction of Tens and Units, and Hundreds, Tens and Units. For example, if the child is faced with $47 + 17$ he is encouraged to think of this (regroup) as a set of $(40 + 7)$ added to a set of $(10 + 7)$. The tens are quickly collected together to make 50, and the two 7's to make 14. Finally 14 put with the 50 is obviously 64. Fewer errors seem to occur with this method than with the 'carry the ten under the line' type of vertical addition; and it is meaningful, does help to develop insight into the structure of number and can be demonstrated in concrete terms.

With subtraction the procedure may be illustrated thus:

$53 - 27$ 53 can be regarded as $(40 + 13)$; and 27 as $(20 + 7)$.
$(40 + 13) - (20 + 7)$
20 (dealing with the tens first) 6 (from $13 - 7$)
We are left with 26.

Once the method is established with understanding it appears to result in fewer errors than either the 'decomposition' or 'equal addition' methods, and it does have more meaning for the child. Equal addition, once considered to be the best method for tackling more difficult subtraction problems, has fallen out of favour since it is difficult to demonstrate the procedure in concrete terms.

(vi) *Fractions*. An appreciation of fractional parts must be taught from concrete materials, not limited to jam tarts and cakes cut into pieces! Philip & Tacey market some useful apparatus under the headings *Visual fractions apparatus* and *Decimal fractions matching sets*. Much can also be taught from structural apparatus, particularly that which is not marked with unit divisions *(Cuisenaire* and *Colour factor)*.

(vii) *The ability to halve and to double numbers.* If this is weak it usually means that the child has had insufficient experience in this type of process. The implications are obvious.

(viii) *Tables.* The vexed question of tables remains unanswered in the mind of many teachers—'Should we teach these by rote? Has that not gone out of fashion? Certainly the importance placed upon 'knowing your tables' has been greatly played down in recent years; but it is still helpful if a child knows multiplication bonds as habit responses. The most positive stand to take where the least able are are concerned is this: if they can quite clearly demonstrate that they understand the structure of a particular table through using structural apparatus, and if they can record their results from this, rather than spend an unwarranted amount of time in committing the table to memory it is better to introduce a table square for quick reference.

Some games (such as *Tables progress games* from Philip & Tacey) help to give practice in remembering multiplication bonds.

(ix) *Money.* It must be stressed that proficiency in dealing quickly and efficiently with money matters is the most important skill for social competence; and although introduced much earlier, it should play an increasingly important part in the programme for the older slow learner. There is no substitute for real-life shopping and budgeting experiences, and these should be used whenever the opportunity arises. With younger children games can help to develop this ability: Galt produces *Banker* and *Buy-a-toy;* Philip & Tacey market *Let's go shopping;* E. J. Arnold offer *New penny pocket money, Shop around, Check and Change, Sum-it* and *Mr. Money;* the *First mathematics decimal money workcards* from Hamish Hamilton are useful. Much valuable free material on School Banks and Savings can be obtained from National Savings Commitee, Alexandra House, Kingsway, London.

(x) *Measuring.* The ability to use a ruler and tape to measure length is reasonably important in life. Care must be taken with the least able that unreasonable degrees of accuracy are not demanded in fine metric measures. It is helpful, of course, to include measuring and constructing of lines and figures in the practical aspects of a mathematics programme; and this kind of activity lends itself well to assignment sheet work. However, far more experience must be provided in measuring in a more meaningful context—curtain lengths, size of angle-brackets to take a shelf, length of wood required for a shelf, length of nails and screws for a particular job, height of a room to be papered, etc.

(xi/xii) *Multiplication and division.* In the surveys which have been carried out to determine adult needs in terms of arithmetic, multiplication and division do not appear to be of great importance.[3][11] Certainly it is useful to be able to multiply, say, 23 lengths of wallpaper by 7 feet to find out how much to order, but the adult who has difficulty with multiplication will usually do it correctly as an addition ·(setting down 23 seven times and adding). For the brighter child who is specifically backward in arithmetic, it may be necessary to teach multiplication diagnostically through the use of structural apparatus and the collecting together of equal sets until understanding replaces a misunderstood and misapplied trick. Similarly, division must be taught in concrete ways with recording being introduced meaningfully alongside real sharing operations.

(xiii) *Telling the time.* See PHASE III comments above.

Again readers are reminded to refer to the books already mentioned to obtain suggestions for a complete maths course for the slow learner.

Suggestions for further study

(a) Examine some of the books and workcards listed in Appendix 8. To what extent would the material need to be modified or adapted before it could be used with pupils of low reading attainment?

(b) For your own class design a set of workcards using a very limited reading vocabulary. The cards should aim to provide practice with money, linear measurement or time.

(c) Discuss with other teachers the possible content of a mathematics syllabus for slow learning junior or secondary pupils.

(d) How important do you consider games to be in the teaching of basic number? Are number games still appropriate for the older pupils at secondary school level?

References

1. ABELWHITE, R. (1969) *Mathematics and the less able,* London, Heinemann.
2. BEILIN, H. (1972) 'The status and future of preschool compensatory education', in STANLEY J. C. (ed.) *Preschool programmes for the disadvantaged,* London and Baltimore, John Hopkins Press.
3. BELL, P. (1970) *Basic teaching for slow learners,* London, Muller.
4. CRONBACH, L.J. (1965) 'Issues current in educational psychology', in Morrisett,L. and Vinsonhaler, J. (eds.) *Mathematical learning,* Society for Reasearch in Child Development Monograph 30, Chicago, University of Chicago Press.
5. FLETCHER, H. (1970) *Mathematics for schools: Teacher's resource book,* London and Reading, Mass., Addison-Wesley.
6. HUGHES, J. M. (1973) *The slow learner in your class,* London, Nelson.
7. IRVING, J. (1972) 'Mathematics for the slow learner', in CROUCH B. (ed.) *Overcoming learning difficulties,* London, Benn.
8. MARSH, L. G. (1969) *Children explore mathematics,* London, Black.
9. Nuffield Mathematics Project (1967) *Mathematics begins,* London, Chambers and Murray.
10. TANSLEY, A. E. and GULLIFORD, R. (1960) *The education of slow learning children,* London, Routledge.
11. THOMPSON, G. E. (1963) 'An arithmetic scheme for ESN children based on their after school needs', *The Slow Learning Child,* **10,** 109–7.
12. WILLIAMS, A. A. (1964) 'Arithmetic at the crossroads', *Special Education,* **53,** 5–10.
13. WILLIAMS, A. A. (1970) *Basic subjects for the slow learner,* London, Methuen.
14. WILLIAMS, P. (1965) 'Notation and Number Difficulties', *Special Education,* **54,** 2–1.

Recommended reading (in addition to titles above)

Association of Teachers of Mathematics (1969) *Notes on mathematics in primary schools,* Cambridge, Cambridge University Press.

BIGGS, E. (1970) *Mathematics for young children,* London, Macmillan.

BIGGS, E. (1973) *Mathematics for the older children,* London, Macmillan.

COPELAND, R. W. (1970) *How children learn mathematics,* London, Macmillan.

DIENES, Z. (1973) *The six stages in the process of learning mathematics,* Slough, NFER.

ISSACS, N. (1960) *New light on children's ideas of number,* London, Ward Lock.

MACDONALD, T. H. (1973) *Basic mathematics and remedial instruction,* Sydney and London, Angus & Robertson.

Nuffield Mathematics Project Guides, *Computation and structure, Environmental geometry, Into secondary school, Mathematics in the later primary years,* London, Murray and Chambers.

PETERSON, D. (1973) *Functional mathematics for the mentally retarded,* Columbus, Ohio, Merrill.

SCHONELL, F. J. (1957) *Diagnosis and remedial teaching in arithmetic,* Edinburgh, Oliver & Boyd.

Symposium on Arithmetic Teaching (1962) *The Slow Learning Child,* **8** and **9.**

Symposium on Maths for the Slow Learner (1968) *Remedial Education,* **3.**

WHITWORTH, D. and EDWARDS, M. (1969) *Teaching mathematics to the ordinary pupil,* London, University of London Press.

WILLIAMS, J. D. (1971) *Teaching Technique in Primary Mathematics* Slough, NFER.

13. Matters of organisation: the provision of special education in the ordinary school

Special Education is often thought of as something that is provided only in special schools. This is quite untrue. *Special Education* is simply education that is specially adapted to meet the child's needs. If these needs can be fully met within the ordinary primary or secondary school so much the better.[9]

Some general points

The current trend in terms of provision is reflected in the statement, '[there is] a growing belief among educationists that children who are handicapped or disadvantaged in some way, ... whether mentally, physically, or socially, ... should wherever possible be educated in a normal rather than a special school' (p.1).[16] This is not new; it was implicit in the 1944 Education Act and explicit in the regulations and circulars which followed it. If one wants to pinpoint the most serious lack of development in the thirty odd years since the Act it is the failure to expand and improve the provision for slow learning children in the ordinary school. Much remains to be done.

Brennan has said, 'The backward child who does not enter a special school is left in the most hazardous situation in the whole of the education system. His educational future is at the mercy of completely fortuitous local circumstances which may differ not only from area to area but from school to school, or even from term to term within the same school'.[5] This is not to imply that a very slow learner is necessarily better off for being placed in a special school. What little research has been done to compare children placed in special schools with similar children remaining in remedial departments fails to demonstrate any overriding supremacy of the former either in academic standards or later social competence.[2 13 19] The indications have been in favour of ordinary school placement even though the provision there frequently leaves much to be desired. The stigma of having been to a special school can be a very real one, although teachers in such schools tend to deny that this is so. Staples[20] suggests that the humiliation of having to admit to workmates or boyfriend that you went to a special school may be a greater and longer-term humiliation than having to experience some learning difficulties in the ordinary school.

If the standard and scope of special educational help within the ordinary school could only be improved it would probably meet the needs of quite a number of children currently referred for special schooling, as well as more adeqately catering for the needs of slow learners already in the normal school.

It is reasonable to ask at this point 'What is special about special educational treatment in the ordinary primary or secondary school?' The several answers to the question will affect organisation.

All forms of special educational help are characterised by:

(i) A greater attention to individual needs and individual differences in ability and experience.

(ii) Modification, sometimes drastic modification, of methods of instruction—a diagnostic approach to teaching.

(iii) Active rather than passive involvement in learning situations.

(iv) A rethinking of the suitability and relevance of the subject matter and skills taught.

(v) The setting of tangible, meaningful, short-term objectives.

(vi) Frequent and regular assessments of progress made, together with appropriate record keeping.

(vii) Greater attention to the all-round development of the child (social, emotional, moral and aesthetic, as well as academic).

(viii) Special expertise, enthusiasm and personality characteristics on the part of the teacher.

As was indicated and defined in chapter 2, 'Special education' is a general term and may be subdivided into four categories, although these should be viewed as emphases rather than clear-cut types of provision: *Adaptive, Compensatory, Remedial, Therapeutic* (see page 16).

Present conditions and problems in the schools, future trends in the placement of handicapped children, and the eight characteristics of special educational help listed above combine to yield the following direct implications for organisation:

(i) In almost every school there will be a number of pupils who need adaptive education; that is, almost every aspect of the curriculum will be modified to meet their needs and a different methodology employed in their instruction. They will need special provision in terms of accommodation, equipment, and staff wherever the number involved justifies it. Where the number involved does not provide a unit viable in its own right, special consideration will have to be given to catering for their needs within the normal class.

(ii) There will be a somewhat larger group of children who need special help with only some aspects of basic skill learning. Their needs can be met either within the normal class or through withdrawal from the class for special group work, or through allocation to a special 'set' for that subject. They may require compensatory as well as remedial help in some cases.

(iii) There will be a few children of average or above average mental ability who have specific learning problems associated with language, reading, writing, spelling or mathematics, and who require special help. In the secondary schools this may include children in the academic streams. Sometimes this need for remedial help can only be met by individual tuition.

Running through the three coarse groupings above will be the need for *therapeutic* help for some pupils.

It is now relevant to consider some patterns of school organisation.

Organisation within the school

The infant school.

In an increasing number of infant schools the patterns of organisation seem designed to work against the needs of the least able pupils and place them more at risk. For example, with the current enthusiasm for open-plan, integrated day, vertically-grouped, progressive primary schools the opportunity to pay more than lip-service to the eight components of special educational help can become extremely difficult. Some would argue that this is not so, that freer approaches allow greater attention to all individuals; but with the present large classes there is not much evidence of the least able receiving special help. The role of the teacher has tended to become increasingly that of an 'organiser of the learning environment' and less that of a teacher. This is not an argument against modern methods of organisation, which are so obviously right for children who are capable of independent learning under general stimulation and guidance with a little help and corrective feedback from the teacher. It is, however, a warning that slow learners and children with specific learning difficulties need special help; and if the pattern of day-to-day organisation and deployment of staff does not allow for regular systematic teaching of such children it is glossing over or ignoring a principal responsibility.

The need for early detection of children with learning problems in the infant school was stressed in chapter 1; and some suitable activities for such children were described in chapters 8 and 9. Children who are not making normal progress can be detected by the second year of their infant schooling. Sometimes all that is necessary is to help the child to adjust to school and to form a friendship.

No one would wish to suggest that infants not making normal progress should be segregated. The special help needed should be provided by setting aside a regular time each day when either the child's own teacher, or a teacher deployed for that purpose within a team teaching situation, can plan and implement appropriate readiness and teaching programmes. Where part-time or supernumerary teachers are employed in the school they are not necessarily the best people to use for remedial or special teaching, unless they are already experienced primary teachers or have followed some in-service training course to equip them for the work. In some situations it is better to use such teachers for other work with larger groups and classes so releasing the class teacher to do the special work with her own slow learners. Some schools favour taking the group of children to receive special help out of the class; others prefer that the extra teacher go into the classroom and work with the group in that setting. Such matters are for internal decision.

In many infant and junior schools more special-group work could be done if the head teacher actually taught for a few periods each week.

The junior school

Some junior schools in favoured catchment areas may not have a serious remedial and compensatory education problem. It may be that difficulties which do arise can be dealt with entirely by the class teacher through careful planning of the working day (see also pages 166–73: and the books by West[21] and Dean[8]). In other schools, with only slightly larger problems, it may be that the regular withdrawal or extraction of a few children from various classes for extra help in basic subjects will meet the need adequately. The groups may be taken by a member of the school staff, a part-time teacher or a visiting peripatetic remedial teacher. The role of visiting remedial teachers is changing in many authorities, and they now tend to provide an advisory service in addition to, or instead of, a teaching service. In either case, it is important that if a teacher other than the child's own class teacher provides help there should be liaison between the two so that the work and suitable activities recommended for the child ensure continuity.

In some junior schools in socially and economically depressed areas the need for special educational help of all kinds may be very great. Two parallel forms of provision are usually necessary—group withdrawal for some pupils, plus special class provision for the least able.

Two junior school systems are summarised in the two tables presented below:

SCHOOL A 185 on roll.

Form J 1. 1st year mixed-ability class, 38 on roll.

Form J 2. 2nd year mixed-ability class, 36 on roll.

Form J 3. Combined 1st/2nd year special class, 20 on roll.

Form J 4. 3rd year mixed-ability class, 37 on roll.

Form J 5. 4th year mixed-ability class, 36 on roll.

Form J 6. Combined 3rd/4th year special class, 18 on roll.

Two teachers are involved full-time with the two special classes except for music and games. The head teacher takes forms for these subjects and so releases the teachers for remedial group work in lower juniors.

SCHOOL B 164 on roll (with infant department on same campus).

Form J 1. Special transition class for all top infants/lower juniors with learning difficulties.

Form J 2. Normal 1st year mixed-ability class, 36 on roll.

Form J 3. Normal 2nd year mixed-ability class, 38 on roll.

Form J 4. Normal 3rd year mixed-ability class, 35 on roll.

Form J 5. Normal 4th year mixed-ability class, 40 on roll.

Special class J1 joins with J2 for music, games and P. E. The head teacher takes the class daily for 'Story' thus releasing the remedial teacher for reading group sessions with pupils in need of help from the second year upwards.

Special classes within the junior/middle/secondary school

In schools with a special educational need of any appreciable size it is usually useful to create a special class, provided that the teacher taking such a class has faith in it as a viable unit. When such classes fail it is almost always because the teacher in charge does not believe in what he/she is attempting to do—perhaps does not believe that some degree of segregation is necessary for the non-literate child—or is attempting to provide special help with no allocation of money for equipment and books, and in unsuitable accommodation. The problem is well stated in the Plowden Report: 'to be educated in an unsatisfactory remedial class can be the worst arrangement of all for a slow learner. The danger of a remedial class or group becoming a place from which none escape and which perpetuates a sense of failure and hopelessness ought to be recognised' (para. 852).[17] Other dangers in creating a special class will be considered in a moment; but first, it is more useful to delineate the positive advantages in such provision since they out-weigh the disadvantages. Also, it should be added, most schools of any size need remedial reading groups in addition to the special class provision—it is not an either-or question.

The advantages of a special class or classes are:

(i) Children who need adaptive education are more likely to receive this in a special class (or, if the school is streamed, in the bottom stream). It is much easier to plan a meaningful programme and to employ suitable methods if the children are brought together to form a viable unit.

(ii) Children with major learning difficulties need to be with one teacher for much of the time, a teacher who gets to know them well and sets levels of expectation and standards which are realistic in the light of the child's problems. Such a teacher is likely to be consistent in her handling of the group and this engenders a feeling of security. This is usually the situation at primary level, but it is rarely found in the post-primary levels where subject-specialisation is the main aim.

(iii) The teacher of a special class will find it easier to teach diagnostically and to make the work suit the child.

(iv) Slow learners don't readily cross subject barriers. Having a class for most of the time means that the teacher can integrate the work in a meaningful way. Again, this is already done at primary level but rarely at the secondary level.

(v) Having your own form base, a place which is 'yours' adds to the feeling of security and belonging and stability referred to above. Many slow learners at secondary level have no firm base but change from room to room for almost every period on the time-table.

(vi) Almost all aspects of the adapted curriculum can, if the teacher wishes, become the vehicle through which to improve basic skills of oracy, literacy and numeracy.

(vii) In a special class situation it is much easier to do more than pay lip-service to the idea of improving social adjustment and developing independence. Children who are isolated and rejected in the peer group, or who are lacking in confidence, can be helped to integrate by careful allocation to work groups where they can make some contribution and the manipulation of social situations to enable the children to show their worth. That the least able pupils do tend to have problems of acceptance within the peer group has been noted elsewhere.[22]

(viii) A special class should be small, with an absolute maximum of 20 pupils.

Ideally, a special class will contain pupils of one age group only; the creation of a special class containing pupils from a wide age range leaves much to be desired, and should be avoided if at all possible. At junior level it is possible to group two years together (1st/2nd or 3rd/4th years) but again, it is not really recommended. Mixed age classes in the secondary school should be avoided.

If any teacher still has doubts about the value of special class provision they should read the book by Davie[7] and *Survey 17* from the Department of Education and Science.[11]

The dangers inherent in creating a special class may be summarised as:

(i) The problem of 'stigma'. To many teachers any form of segregation is very undesirable: such teachers might remember the statement, 'A child cannot be more cruelly segregated than to be placed in a room where his failures separate him from other children who are experiencing success' (p. 99).[6]

Actually, when the least able pupils are catered for separately, the efficient teaching of mixed-ability groups both at primary and lower secondary levels becomes a much more viable proposition. There seems little point in finely streaming able and average children; the problems emerge when non-literate or semi-literate children are to be taught in large mixed-ability classes which also contain some extremely able pupils. If an increasing number of ESN children are to be contained in the ordinary school the need for special classes is likely to increase also.

Although a special class is bound to be recognised for what it is both by the pupils within and outside, at least it can be treated within the school as just another class. It should be numbered or lettered along with the rest, not referred to as the special class', 'the progress class', 'the opportunity class', 'the remedials', 'the remove' or as the present writer's first class in a large secondary school was known, 'lower 13'. The teacher should also strive to build kudos in the class in ways which are respected by other classes: 'the form that built the canoe during the lunch hours'; 'the form that won the basket ball competition'; 'the class which runs its own disco'; 'the classroom where you are allowed to use the teaching machines and the tape recorder'.

The special class or unit (and equally the teacher) should never become isolated.

(ii) The special class may become the dumping ground for all the school's 'misfits'. Some misfits do belong in the special class if their problems stem from limited ability and poor background; but others, bright but very troublesome children, do not belong in the class.

(iii) The creation of a special class may tie the remedial specialist down too much to one small group. This should not happen; and need not, as the time-table on page 169 indicates.

(iv) The class may be 'special' in name only—no extra money for special equipment or suitable accommodation provided.

(v) A special class can appear on paper to have solved the special education problem in the school; but may actually leave twice as many pupils in need of help outside the group as within it. Hence the question 'shall we have a special class or shall we have a system of group withdrawal?' is not an either/or matter; as was stated earlier, in most schools with any appreciable problem both forms of provision are required.

(vi) There is a danger that the standard of work expected from the children may gradually decline if the teacher in charge never has contact with any children making normal progress.[11] It is easy for the teacher to forget just how much bright children can produce virtually unaided.

(vii) At secondary level the special class time-table should not prevent the pupils from having very beneficial contact with some subject specialists, for instance in art, drama, music, domestic science, even though these areas may also be integrated already into some of the special class programme.

(viii) If a pupil is wrongly placed in a special class and is not transferred for several terms, it becomes increasingly impossible, at the secondary level, for him to pick up the threads of some subject syllabus which has been followed by the main streams.

Streaming children by ability and attainment in the primary school is rapidly disappearing as an administrative practice, mixed-ability classes now being favoured. However, some junior schools do still stream, and many more secondary schools still adopt it as their pattern of organisation. The bottom stream more or less equates with a special class in each year; it does, however, tend to be larger than the prescribed 20 pupils, but as far as possible should be kept small to allow for the provision of special educational help.

Special educational help at secondary (post-primary) level

At secondary level there exists a very real problem, aggravated in many schools by the pattern of organisation which stresses subject-specialisation and ignores the learning difficulties of some of the pupils. The present writer has no hesitation in describing some secondary schools as grave-yards of human potential for the non-academic child. The lack of consideration of the needs of slow learning secondary children in some areas and schools is tantamount to a local if not a national scandal. The point is well put in the Department of Education and Science Survey 15,[10] 'A number of schools involved their slow learners, at least for the first year or two, in a common curriculum ... the effects were often unfortunate and in a few cases disastrous. The ability range in some classes often posed intractable teaching problems; extreme specialisation exposed the slow learners (and maybe the not-so-slow learners) to too many changes of teachers (in one instance as many as 14, for even single subjects like English were sometimes subdivided among several teachers), none of whom had sufficient time (and not all had sufficient interest) to get to know the needs of the slowest pupils in the round. In some cases pupils with barely the rudiments of literacy (in a few instances not even that) were bored and bewildered in all lessons demanding the use of books. Both time-table and curriculum were fragmented to the point of being incomprehensible to the least able pupils. Arrangements such as these constitute not equality of opportunity but a denial of opportunity, a denial of opportunity for successful achievement' (p.25).[10]

The H.M.I.'s who conducted this enquiry found that only 51 schools in a sample of 158 had a special department to deal with special educational needs. Even when 'remedial departments' exist they may exist in name only, and close observation within the school fails to reveal any positive approach to tackle the problems of the least able. In other cases (relatively few) one does find a well-structured department with wide terms of reference offering a variety of special help. Such departments are beginning to shed the title 'Remedial Department' in favour of 'Department of General Education', or 'Department of Basic Studies'; and why not, if it helps to improve the image?

At the secondary school level, and at different stages within the secondary course, various systems are advocated including the following variations:

(i) *Streaming* This implies that the children are sorted into class units on the basis of ability and/or achievement, the more able pupils being placed in 'top streams' and the least able in 'low streams'. It was found to be the most common form of organisation in the survey referred to above.

Streaming as a procedure has developed certain unpleasant associations due largely to research findings which suggest that a child once 'branded' with a stream or grade label will eventually oblige by performing at that level regardless of his potential.[3][12][14] However, in many secondary schools the provision of a remedial stream (not called by that title) is no bad thing provided that it is taken for much of the time by a suitable teacher, and in other ways conforms with the special class outlined above. It is certainly to be preferred to some superficial and inefficient attempt at creating mixed-ability forms with teachers who do not expect the system to work successfully even before its implementation.

(ii) *Broad banding* This term usually implies a coarser division of the year groups into 'A' and 'B' bands, which in a six-form entry school may contain three forms each. The 'A' band contains children of average and above average ability, while the 'B' band caters for the children who are average and below. Broad banding may also have running through it a system of subject sets and/or withdrawal or extraction of pupils for special help.

(iii) *Mixed-ability grouping* This pattern of organisation is becoming more popular, largely because of the reactions to streaming referred to above. Provided it is well organised, mixed-ability grouping can present a very stimulating situation in which to teach and to learn. Usually the system is restricted to the first two years of the post-primary course, giving way to some form of setting or optional courses in the upper school.

Some mixed-ability systems fail because the class is not taken by one teacher for several periods and subjects on the time-table. To send a mixed-ability class to different subject specialists for almost every subject never allows a teacher to get to know individuals within the group, yet this is the pre-requisite for successful teaching across a range of ability. Mixed-ability classes are not infrequently 'streamed internally' through the creation of work groups which clearly reflect different ability levels within the class; this would appear to defeat the object of the whole exercise.

Mixed-ability grouping may also have running through it a system of group extraction for special help; or remedial teachers may supply special help within the classroom, working in partnership with the class teacher for some periods in the week. This has the advantage of linking the special help with the normal on-going class work. Unfortunately, not all teachers are able or disposed to work in partnership in this way.

(iv) *Subject setting* This system is much favoured in many schools as it avoids the clear-cut segregation which streaming or special classes may seem to present. Pupils are allocated to sets according to their ability in a particular subject. It usually requires fairly extensive 'block time-tabling' (so that up to six or seven sets can all have mathematics at the same time, or three sets can always have mathematics at the same time that three other sets take another subject, etc.). It can, but need not, destroy the 'class' as a viable social unit, create a sense of 'not belonging' to any teacher, and it may separate mutual friendships.

(v) *House groups or tutor groups* In some schools one finds the odd practice of having groups which meet only for purposes of regis-tration then dissolve and go separate ways in sets, bands and streams for the working day. The teacher in charge is theoretically supposed to have pastoral care of the children within the group; but he is unlikely even to know many of them unless he also teaches them. The children sometimes lack a form-base with which they can iden-tify; they may even lack a desk or a locker and be compelled to carry with them all items required for the day's lessons. This probably describes the most inappropriate system from the point of view of the least able, who need security and stability above all else.

(vi) *Team teaching* This is not necessarily an alternative form of organisation but an approach which may be used from time to time within any of the existing systems. It gives teachers the experience of co-operating and working together as a team, each making a useful contribution from his or her own particular skills, yet at the same time widening and increasing their own expertise. It is an approach which allows not only barriers between subject areas to be broken down, but also barriers between streams, sets or classes.

It is beyond the scope of this Handbook to describe in detail the operation of various forms of team teaching. It will suffice to illustrate the connection with remedial and special help by giving an example.

In a secondary school with a six-form entry and a special class the whole of the first year age group (including the special class) are block time-tabled for ten to twelve periods per week for a project lasting a fortnight. Seven teachers (including the remedial teacher) are made available to form the team, and the success of the project depends entirely upon very careful planning by them beforehand. Give and take and compromise are always necessary in the pre-planning. Appropriate resource materials, audio-visual aids, must be gathered together, visits arranged, group work planned and, if necessary, speakers from outside the school booked for certain times. The planning needs to be so thorough that at most only one team teaching project should be attempted in each half term. It is probably true to say that the biggest single obstacle to team teaching is the difficulty encountered in attempting to get seven teachers to co-operate! (See fig. 4)

(vii) *Other systems* and variations of the six presented here are described in articles in *Remedial Education*.[14][15][18][23]

It is easy to be critical of special educational provision in the secondary school, but the inherent problems in many systems reflect difficulties in staffing, accommodation, finance and the rightful demands of the academic as well as the non-academic pupils. Head teachers have differing philosophies and may believe very firmly in the policy which they implement. It is not possible to prescribe the perfect system of special educational treatment at secondary level—too many variables are involved. However, on page 163 a pattern is presented which is applicable (with modification) to many secondary schools. One assumption has to be made: the general

Fig 4. *Example – Remedial work linked with team teaching.*

Theme 'Communications'. 10–12 periods per week for two weeks.
6 classes + special class. 7 teachers (including remedial teacher).

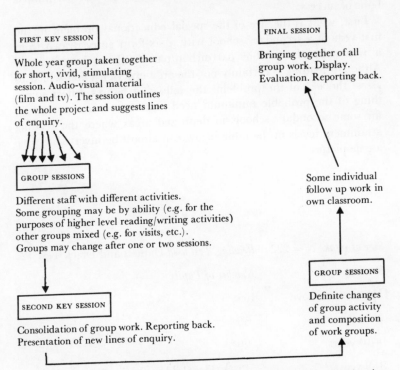

The remedial teacher advises on content for the less able pupils at the planning
stages and also takes a group at all group sessions (but not necessarily one of low
ability). The less able pupils are integrated for as much of the programme as possible. The remedial teacher also links basic skill work related to the project during
class lessons, and in this way even the special class are able to present written
work in the final exhibitions and display.

pattern of organisation within the school must allow for such provision by giving it reasonably high priority when the annual timetable is devised. If special education is merely slotted into the spare spaces on an otherwise complete time-table then there is limited hope of success.

First, what is the size of the special educational problem in the first year of a secondary school with a six-form entry drawn from a reasonably favourable part-urban/part-rural catchment area? Although reading is certainly not the only criterion upon which to assess the size of the problem, the following figures reflect something of the probable minimum need. The figures are unrealistic for some secondary schools in depressed areas where the reading attainment levels in the table below can almost be inverted to give a true picture.

Size of intake N = 222   *Reading Test used* Daniels and Diack Test 12.

Reading Ages	*Number of Pupils*	
$11\frac{1}{2}$ years or above	106	
$10–11\frac{1}{2}$ years	56	
9–10 years	29*	
8–9 years	13	The children in these categories definitely require special help with reading and written language, some also with mathematics. Total not less than 31. Approximately 18 candidates for a special class.
7–8 years	6	
6–7 years	7	
Below 6 years	5	

* These 29 pupils comprise an 'at risk' group in secondary schools. Their measured reading age usually means that they do not receive any form of help with reading (they are deemed 'functionally literate') yet they cannot cope with most secondary school textbooks. The English specialist may not perceive their need to develop reading skills and hence these pupils may leave at the end of a secondary course with a reading age equivalent to that at entry. It is pupils like these who benefit from such material as the SRA, *Reading laboratories* and the Ward Lock *Workshop 9–13*, and such material can be put in the hands of the English specialist.

PATTERN OF PROVISION WITHIN A SECONDARY SCHOOL
(before raising of school leaving age to sixteen years)

Note No day special school for educationally subnormal children in the area so the school contains a higher than average number of ESN children.

Deployment of staff	*Remedial help through extraction from normal classes*
1st Year (N = 222) Six mixed-ability classes plus one special class (n = 20)	20 pupils.
2nd Year Six mixed-ability groups plus one special class (n = 12)	18 pupils*
3rd Year †Six classes only, sets for most subjects. (lowest set)	8 pupils‡
4th Year Course options with sets for maths and language skills. (lowest set)	6 pupils‡
5th Year Examination courses (GCE/CSE)	Tutorial help for a few selected individuals in spelling and maths.

Staff in special education department

1 Head of department with specialist qualifications in remedial education. He takes first year special class for 24 periods per week; and basic English and mathematics with the bottom set third year for 10 periods per week.

* This group of 18 pupils contains some who were transferred from a special class at the end of the first year but still need help in basic skill subjects.
† Block time-table for work in sets.
‡ These pupils in third and fourth years are the ESN children of limited ability who require extra support, both teaching and counselling, throughout their school life.

1 Remedial teacher (full-time) takes second year special class for 18 periods per week; and basic English and mathematics with the bottom set in the fourth year for 10 periods. She also takes 6 periods of remedial group work per week (extraction from normal classes).

1 Part-time teacher (mornings only) takes 18 periods per week of remedial reading and mathematics (extraction groups from normal classes).

OTHER POSSIBLE PATTERNS OF PROVISION AND DEPLOYMENT OF STAFF

These do not relate to the school presented in detail above.

(i) One specialist available for 33 periods per week
    1st year Special class 19 periods
    2nd year Lower stream or set 5 periods on language skills
                            4 periods on number/maths skills
    3rd/4th year Withdrawal groups 4 periods

(ii) One specialist available 33 periods per week
    1st/2nd year Special class 19 periods per week
                Withdrawal groups 5 periods per week
    3rd year Lower stream or set 5 periods on language skills
    4th year Withdrawal groups 4 periods per week

(iii) One specialist available for 33 periods per week
    1st/2nd year Special class for 20 periods per week
    3rd/4th year Withdrawal groups for 13 periods per week

(iv) One specialist available for 30 periods per week. No special class
    1st year Lower stream or set 8 periods on language skills
                            6 periods on number/maths skills
    2nd year Lower stream or set 8 periods on language skills
                            4 periods on mathematics
    Upper school Remedial groups 4 periods only for least able

(v) Two remedial specialists available for 30 periods per week each

1st year Special class	20 periods	}	Teacher A
1st year Remedial groups	10 periods		
2nd year Special class	18 periods	}	Teacher B
2nd year Remedial groups	6 periods		
3rd/4th year Groups	6 periods		

(vi) Two remedial specialists: Teacher A = 30 periods;
                                Teacher B = 20 periods.
    1st/2nd year Special class 20 periods

3rd year	Lower English set	6 periods	}	Teacher A
	Lower maths set	4 periods	}	
1st year	Remedial groups	6 periods	}	
2nd year	Remedial groups	6 periods	}	Teacher B
Upper school	Remedial groups	8 periods	}	

What are the terms of reference for a remedial department?

To provide a system of special educational help (adaptive, compensatory, remedial and therapeutic) within the school, making opptimum use of remedial teaching staff and providing optimum coverage for the pupils in need. This may involve both special class work and work with groups or individuals extracted from normal classes. It will embrace counselling and liaison as well as teaching.

What is the role of the head of the remedial department?

(i) To assess the nature and extent of the special educational needs within the school, and keep regular checks on the situation throughout the five school years.

(ii) To plan, in collaboration with the head teacher, a system of special educational help to meet the needs of the school.

(iii) Diagnosis and assessment of children's learning problems; planning of appropriate lines of remediation; advising other teachers of suitable methods and materials.

(iv) To keep detailed records on each child receiving special help, (see below).

(v) Liaison with heads of departments covering all school subjects—mainly an advisory role suggesting necessary modification to subject syllabus, etc.

(vi) Within a mixed-ability situation, responsibility for notifying general subjects teachers and subject specialists of children with learning difficulties, their needs and their limitations.

(vii) Responsibility for calling in help from outside agencies (School Psychological Service, school medical officer, etc.) when this appears necessary in order to help certain individuals.

(viii) Pastoral care of the least able pupils throughout the school course.

(ix) Drawing up 'departmental policy'. The calling of regular departmental meetings at which general problems may be discussed and specific children considered in detail. These 'case conferences' should at times involve other teachers who are having problems with a particular maladjusted child. It is vital that all staff teaching the child adopt a common pattern of reaction to the child's behaviour, and avoid diversity ranging from the very permissive to the extremely strict.

(x) Liaison with parents, careers master or careers officer at time of school leaving.

(xi) In some schools the responsibility for all forms of testing and assessment throughout the school falls upon the remedial department head.

(xii) The head of remedial department should have some say in the selection and appointment of staff to the department.

Record keeping

It is generally accepted that all teachers need to keep records of pupils' progress and attainments. Too frequently this amounts merely to the recording of a child's marks for particular subjects or pieces of work. Such marks are subsequently totalled for a term or a year, and the child is ranked as good, average or poor on this result. At best, this form of recording serves a very limited purpose. More detailed and personalised recording is necessary within a remedial department.

There are two principal reasons why records need to be kept:

(a) To give an up-to-the-minute picture of a child's present level of achievement, together with some indication of the progress he has made in the past, his particular strengths and weaknesses and his social adjustment. If a teacher is really gearing his instruction to the individual child's needs he just cannot do without such notes and records of progress. These are 'personal' records for the teacher's own reference and guidance.

(b) To provide concise information about the child for the guidance of others (perhaps the head teacher when making a report, the educational psychologist, the school medical officer, the careers master or the school counsellor). In particular such information should be passed on to the next teacher taking the child over in a new class or new school.

The best form of record keeping to meet requirement (a) above is a record book with a thumb-index down the right hand margin. Several pages are set aside for each child at the beginning of the year, and are made available for a cumulative record. The book will contain background information from previous schools, from home visits, from testing and assessment, and a summary of the total implications for teaching. This record book is for the teacher's own reference; it contains too much information, some of it confidential, for general purposes.

To meet requirement (b) above, the head of the remedial department should design a record card or record sheet for use within the department. It should contain appropriate headings and space for a concise summary of only the really relevant information concerning any child who is receiving some form of special help, either in a special class or in a remedial group. These cards will be updated perhaps once a term.

The school record card (usually kept in the head teacher's room or the school office) should have a note attached to it indicating that the child is receiving special help and that up-to-date information is available from current records in the remedial department.

Useful information on record keeping is contained in the little book by Dean.[8]

Classroom organisation

One look at the classroom plan (fig. 5) indicates that the kind of room which is most suitable for work with less able juniors and seniors is not unlike the average infant classroom—but with fewer pupils per square inch! The equipment and surroundings will be more in keeping with the older children's level of maturity and interest.

The absence of desks arranged in formal rows allows greater flexibility for organising group work for much of the time.

Work groups should not be static and permanent; their composition will vary from activity to activity and should certainly not be a form of internal streaming. At times the teacher will organise group work in such a way that the shy, withdrawn child is placed in a group or given a partner where he/she gets the opportunity to achieve at least some success because the situation is not monopolised by more confident, extrovert members of the class.

It is not always essential to use sociometric techniques and the construction of sociograms to determine social relationships within the class; but it is one method which may help to support a

Fig. 5 Special classroom for 18 to 20 pupils.

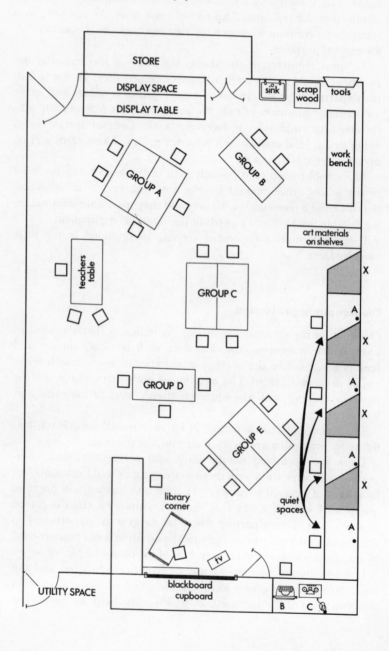

teacher's more subjective judgement concerning isolated and rejected children in the group, particularly at secondary level.[22]

The time-tables (figs. 6 and 7) may help to indicate the programme pursued by the class each day. Fig. 6 shows times when
the special class is not taken by its own teacher, he/she being released
to do other forms of remedial work. Fig. 7, on page 170 indicates the
kind of activities operating at other times.

Fig. 6

M	P.E.				
Tu		R.I.			
W				R.I.	GAMES
Th	HANDICRAFTS & DOMESTIC SCIENCE				MUSIC
F			P.E.		

Looking at the second of the two time-tables (fig. 7), it should be
stressed that there is no need at all to follow the set programme
slavishly from week to week. When the occasion arises the whole
day can be used for quite different purposes, seizing the opportunity
to develop some immediate interest. However, having a structured
programme set out at least does provide a firm basis from which
one can work for most of the time without loosing the chance to
be flexible.

KEY: Fig. 5

A—sockets for headphones. B—typewriter. C— tape recorder.

X—hardboard screens to provide four quiet spaces for individual work.

The tables are flat, formica-top units. Pupils' personal equipment is kept in lockers
in the utility space outside the room. The room is used by the special class for
approximately 24 periods per week. It is also used at other times for remedial group
work and counselling. It is not used by larger mixed-ability classes at any time.

Fig. 7

M		*number activities*	language activities	topic work/environmental studies (usually <u>out</u>)	
Tu	*language activities*		number. Gp A | ART A ART B | number. Gp B	science | BBC drama and mime | free activities	
W	language or number groups. art for some		topic work		
Th				number.Gp A | number.Gp B language.Gp B | language.Gp A	
F	TV club and follow up		number work	free activities. hobbies etc also consolidation of topic work, displays etc	story

Language activities shown on the time-table should involve time spent in talking, reading and writing. The discussion and writing can be very much concerned with the project work, visits, team teaching themes and so on shown at other points on the time-table.

As a rule it is valuable to take a special class out from school at least once each week. Maximum use can be made of the environment within easy walking distance from the school to stimulate interest and to provide meaningful reasons for writing reports, questionnaires, etc.

Again looking at the time-table, *Art* would sometimes be taken as a lesson with the whole class; but at other times it does present an opportunity for some children to get on with minimum supervision while the teacher sits down to work with a group on number skills or language activities (see Tuesday, Wednesday and Thursday on the time-table).

Perhaps *Free activities* requires some explanation. This is a time when children are able to complete unfinished work, to use teaching machine assignments, to listen to pre-recorded stories on tape or to work individually with the teacher. When this is part of the established pattern within the week children do not freely decide to do nothing.

The sections marked with a heavy black line on the time-table indicate times when group work was used to the full, and the teacher was able to circulate and work with groups or individuals.

The fact that *story* appears only on Friday afternoon does not imply that a special class should only be read to once a week. A class like this needs to be read to frequently. But in this particular class, having had a very busy and active Friday afternoon, a story was a suitable and quiet way to end the week, and it became the established pattern.

Much use of display needs to be made in the classroom—models, pictures, maths charts and written work. The fact that the classroom is not used by other larger classes means that such work does not get damaged or defaced.

A suggested list of equipment, apparatus and materials for a special class

EQUIPMENT
1 tape recorder; 6 sets of headphones with extension lead and junction box; 1 typewriter; 1 record player; 2 linear teaching machines; 1 fish tank; 2 cages; 1 vivarium; tv set; woodwork bench or craft table; bookshelves.

TOOLS
1 coping saw; 1 rip saw; 2 tenon saws; 2 hammers; 1 pr pliers; 1 pr pincers; 1 pr tin-snips; 1 large, 1 small screwdriver; 1 rasp; 1 hand drill and bits; 2 wood chisels; nails, screws, nuts/bolts; sandpaper; paint brushes 1″, 1½″, 2″; household paint.

ART MATERIALS
Sugar paper; kitchen paper; coloured gummed papers; powder paint; poster colours; craft knives; paint brushes (various); coloured felt; wire; scissors; modelling clay; paste; glue; pins; balsa wood; long-arm stapler.

FOR REFERENCE
20 copies of street plan of the neighbourhood; 1 copy of *A to Z Street Directory;* 3 copies of *Ordnance Survey map* of the district; bus time-tables; train time-tables; *AA Handbook*; telephone directory.

The group reading lesson

In both the special class situation and the remedial reading group setting it is best if some systematic and planned approach is used for the teaching of reading. Indeed, if any use at all is to be made of chapters 7 to 12 of this book it is essential that the reading session be structured carefully. The diagram (fig. 8) summarises the use of a 30–40 minute period for reading and language skills.

Fig. 8

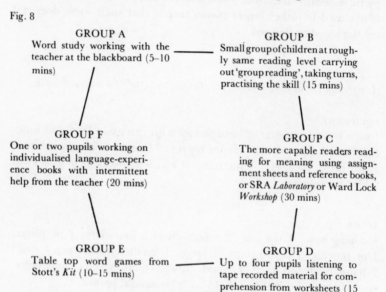

GROUP A
Word study working with the teacher at the blackboard (5–10 mins)

GROUP B
Small group of children at roughly same reading level carrying out 'group reading', taking turns, practising the skill (15 mins)

GROUP F
One or two pupils working on individualised language-experience books with intermittent help from the teacher (20 mins)

GROUP C
The more capable readers reading for meaning using assignment sheets and reference books, or SRA *Laboratory* or Ward Lock *Workshop* (30 mins)

GROUP E
Table top word games from Stott's *Kit* (10–15 mins)

GROUP D
Up to four pupils listening to tape recorded material for comprehension from worksheets (15 mins)

Interchange will take place between groups A, B, D, E—not using the same blackboard material, word games, comprehension work or reading books but a change of activity from one kind to another.

Ten to fifteen minutes per lesson will also be spent in discussion with the teacher or with training in listening skills (including listening to a story read or told by the teacher for the children's enjoyment). Within a week a child should have partaken of at least four different activities in addition to time spent in actually reading to the teacher.

Teachers using this form of organisation for the first time would do well to begin by splitting the class into only two sections for a while, then gradually increasing the number of groups and the range of activities. It will be necessary to use the established pattern fairly regularly once it is accepted, otherwise the pupils will never really acquire the correct work habits and take too long to settle down.

Suggestions for further study

(a) Do you feel that the pattern of organisation in your own school is suitable for meeting the needs of your least able pupils? If not, how would you wish to change it?

(b) Should a Special Education Department, particularly at secondary level, have its own base and resources?

(c) In appointing staff for work with slow learners what type of teacher with what sort of specialisms should the head teacher be seeking?

(d) What is the biggest single obstacle to the efficient provision of special educational help in your school? How might it be overcome?

(e) If one had to present to the headmaster a list of planning priorities for the least able pupils in the school, what would go on to the list?

(f) How might career prospects be improved for teachers wishing to specialise in remedial education?

References

1. ADAMS, A. (1971) 'Some implications of the organisation of secondary schools,' *Remedial Education*, **6**, No. 3, 9–13.
2. ASCHER, M. A. (1970) 'The attainments of children in ESN schools and remedial departments', *Educational Research*, **12**, 215–9.
3. BARKER-LUNN, J. C. (1970) *Streaming in the primary school*, Slough, N.F.E.R.
4. BLACKBURN, S. (1972) 'Westfield Comprehensive School: the slow learners department', *Remedial Education*, **7**, No. 3, 11–3.
5. BRENNAN, W. (1971) 'A policy for remedial education', *Remedial Education*, **6**, No. 1, 7–11.
6. CLEUGH, M. F. (1957) *The slow learner*, London, Methuen.
7. DAVIE, A. (1971) *In a class of their own*, London, Chatto & Windus.
8. DEAN, J. (1972) *Recording children's progress*, London, Macmillan.
9. Department of Education & Science (1965) *Reports on education, No. 23*, London, HMSO.
10. Department of Education & Science (1971) *Slow learners in secondary schools, Survey 15*, London, HMSO.

11. Department of Education & Science (1972) *Aspects of special education: special schools for delicate children and special classes in the ordinary school, Survey 17,* London HMSO.
12. DOUGLAS, J. W. (1964) *The home and the school,* London, MacGibbon & Kee.
13. GREEN, L. F. (1969) 'Comparison of school attainments,' *Special Education,* **58**, 9–12.
14. JACKSON, B. (1964) *Streaming: an education system in miniature,* London, Routledge.
15. KEMP, A. (1971) 'When is a child ready to return to the ordinary class?' *Remedial-Education,* **6**, No. 1, 34–7.
16. N.F.E.R. (1974) *Educational research news, No. 20, Slough,* N.F.E.R.
17. Plowden Report (1967) *Children in the primary school, Vol, I,* London, HMSO.
18. REES DAVIES, E. D. (1969) 'The ability spread of first year students', *Remedial Education,* **4**, No. 4, 203–6.
19. ROBERTSON, J. S. (1963) 'Occupational success of educationally subnormal school leavers', *The Medical Officer, No. 2864.*
20. STAPLES, J. R. (1967) 'Some thoughts on the segregation of educationally subnormal pupils', *Remedial Education,* **2**, No. 11–5.
21. WEST, R. H. (1967) *Organisation in the classroom,* Oxford, Blackwell.
22. WESTWOOD, P. S. (1971) 'Isolated and rejected children', *Remedial Education,* **6**, No. 3, 25–8.
23. Articles by Williams, K., Oakley, R. H., Gordon, M., Mellon, H. (1969) in 'Secondary school symposium', *Remedial Education,* **4**, No. 2, 66–79, and (1974) in *Remedial Education,* **9**, No. 1, 9–21.

Recommended Reading (in addition to books listed above)

BANKS, O. and FINLAYSON, D. (1973) *Success and failure in the secondary school,* London Methuen.

BLACKHAM, G. J. (1967) *The deviant child in the classroom,* Belmont, California, Wadsworth.

Comprehensive Remedial Provision (1977) various authors, *Forum for the Discussion of New Trends in Education* Vol. 19. No.2.

Department of Education & Science (1972) *Children with specific reading difficulties.* London, HMSO.

HAIGH, G. (1977) *Teaching Slow Learners* London, Temple Smith.

HARGREAVES, D. H. (1967) *Social relations in a secondary school,* London, Routledge.

JONES-DAVIES, G. (ed) (1975) *The Slow Learner in the Secondary School* London, Ward Lock.

KING, R. (1973) *School organisation and pupil involvement,* London, Routledge.

PETRIE, C. (1972) *Backward and maladjusted children in secondary schools,* London, Ward Lock.

SCHONELL, F. J. (1962) *The slow learner: segregation or integration?* Queensland University Press.

Schools Council. The following publications are useful: (1967) *Society and the young school leavers;* (1967) *Counselling in schools;* (1968) *Enquiry: young school leavers;* (1970) *Cross'd with adversity;* (1971) *Choosing a curriculum for the young school leaver.* The Schools Council material is published by HMSO prior to 1970, and by Evans and Methuen from 1970.

SIMON, B. and TYNE, A. (1964) *Non-streaming in the junior school,* Leicester, P.S.W. Forum Publications.

TAYLOR, E. A. (1949) *Experiments with a backward class,* London, Methuen.

VARMA, V. P. (1973) *Stresses in children,* London, University of London Press.

WALL, W. D. *et al.* (1962) *Failure in school,* Hamburg, UNESCO.

WARWICK, D. (1971) *Team teaching,* London, University of London Press.

WIDLAKE, P. (1972) *Literacy in the secondary school,* National Association for Remedial Education.

Appendices

Number vocabulary

Many slow learners experience added difficulties in understanding
number work and mathematics because they do not fully understand
some of the words which the teacher uses in explaining situations,
posing problems, or asking questions. The following list contains
words which are frequently used by teachers. If a child is experiencing
very marked difficulties it is necessary to check his/her understanding
of these words, over a period of time, using concrete situations as
far as possible to prove understanding (or lack of it).

QUANTITY and NUMBER

all	same	most	none	large	less than	couple
another	different	least	smaller	larger	share	sort
altogether	enough	other	smallest	largest	double	set
amount	many	small	big	much	twice	group
each	more	few	bigger	several	single	size
equal	more than	little	biggest	less	pair	half (halve)
answer						

LENGTH and MEASUREMENT

length	middle	deep	high	shallow
measure	centre	thick	low	long	far
width	height	thin	narrow	longer ... (est)	corner
across	equal	tall ... est	wide	edge	straight
distance	depth	short ... est	broad	line	side

VOLUME and WEIGHT

heavy	heaviest	light	lightest	weight	empty	full	balance	equal

TIME

days of the week

week	minute	second	year	day	fortnight	month	hour
today	yesterday	tomorrow	morning	afternoon	evening	night	soon
always	fast	slow	slowly	quickly	speed	late	early

SPACE, FORM, AREA

shape	size	straight	round	flat	square	piece	part	strip	line
circle	across	cross	corner	point	angle	curve	curved	edge	
triangle	diamond	pattern	cover	surface					

NOTATION

figure	once	makes	left	odd	even
number	twice	take	equals	add	
take away	three times	from	tens	hundreds	

MONEY

buy	cash	cost	sell	coin	worth	spend	change
cheap	save	price	earn	wages	pay	expensive	names of coins

POSITION

Ordinal values (first, second, etc.)   last   final   middle

between	behind	in front	beside	under	over
next	start	finish	end	above	below
before	outside	inside	forward	backwards	left
right	into	next but one	near	far	close
row	column	after	up	down	sloping

APPENDIX 2

Revised norms for the Vernon revision of the *Burt Graded Word Reading Test* **(1972)**

READING AGE   (Months)

(Years)	0	1	2	3	4	5	6	7	8	9	10	11
5	1	2	3	5	6	8	9	10	11	12	13	14
6	15	16	17	18	20	21	22	23	24	25	26	27
7	28	29	30	32	33	34	35	36	37	38	39	40
8	41	42	44	45	46	47	48	49	50	51	52	53
9	54	56	57	58	59	60	61	62	63	64	65	66
10	68	69	70	71	72	73	74	75	76	77	78	80
11	81											

Reproduced here by kind permission of E. Shearer, Senior Educational Psychologist, Cheshire County Council, these norms are based on results from over 6000 children providing a representative sample.

APPENDIX 3

Norms for the *One Minute Addition* and *One Minute Subtraction Tests* (1974). See Chapter 6.

ADDITION

AGE	5½yr	6yr	6½yr	7yr	7½yr	8yr	8½yr	9yr	9½yr	10yr	10½yr	11yr
Average score	2½	4½	7	10	13½	15½	17½	19	20	21	22	23
* Critical score	0	2	3	6	7	9	12	13	14	15	15	16

SUBTRACTION

AGE	5½yr	6yr	6½yr	7yr	7½yr	8yr	8½yr	9yr	9½yr	10yr	10½yr	11yr
Average score	1	3½	6½	8½	10½	12	13	15	16½	17½	19	21
* Critical score	0	0	3	6	8	9	10	11	12	13	13	14

* By *Critical score* is meant the score below which a child is definitely outside the normal range for his age group. This is a more useful way of viewing a child's result than reading an arithmetic age from a lower group.

APPENDIX 4

Sources of test material

A.C.E.R., Frederick Street, Hawthorn, Victoria, Australia.

Chatto & Windus Ltd, 42 William IV Street, London, W. C. 2.

Education Evaluation Enterprises, Queen Anne House, Queen Square, Bristol, BS1 4AE.

Ginn & Co. Ltd Test Services, Elsinore House, Buckingham Street, Aylesbury, Bucks.

Harrap & Co. Ltd, 182 High Holborn, London, W. C. 1.

Heinemann Educational Ltd, 48 Charles Street, London, WIX 8AH.

H. K. Lewis & Co., Gower Street, London, W. C. 1.

Macmillan & Co. Ltd, Houndmills, Basingstoke.

D. V. Moseley, 294 Park Road, London, N8 8JY. *Blending of phonemes, Discrimination of phonemes* and *P.O.P. spatial tests.*

N.F.E.R. Test Agency, 2 Jennings Buildings, Thames Avenue, Windsor, Berks.

Nelson & Sons Ltd., Lincoln Way, Windmill Road, Sunbury-on-Thames, TW16 7HP.

Oliver & Boyd, Robert Stevenson House, 1–3 Baxter's Place, Leith Walk, Edinburgh EH1 3BB.

Coral Richards, Brookside Cottage, Westbrook Street, Blewbury, Didcot, Berks OX11 QA9. *Tests of understanding the spoken word.*

University of London Press Ltd. (Hodder & Stoughton Educational), Mill Road, Dunton Green, Sevenoaks, Kent TN13 2YA.

APPENDIX 5

Books covering speech development and speech and articulation training

BALDWIN, G. (1967) *Patterns of sound,* London, Chartwell Press.

GODA, S. (1970) *Articulation therapy and consonant drill book,* London and N.Y., Grune & Stratton.

HAMPSON, M. (1969) *Sounds and rhythm,* (3 books + manual), London, Ginn.

VAN RIPER, C. (1963) *Speech correction: principles and methods* (4th Ed.), London, Constable.

WILLIAMS, R. (1962) *Speech difficulties in childhood,* London, Harrap.

See also the journal *British Journal of Disorders of Communication,* Longman Group.

Books covering the teaching of handwriting

INGLIS, A. and GIBSON, E. H. (1970) *The teaching of handwriting,* teacher's books and pupil's books for infant and junior levels, London, Nelson.

RICHARDSON, M. *Writing and writing patterns,* London, University of London Press.

Precept shadow letter tracing sheets (R72), *Matrix script letter guide* and *First* and *Second script writing books* (R142–1 and 2), Philip & Tacey Ltd.

Books covering the selection of materials for backward pupils

ATKINSON, E. J. and GAINS, C. W. (1973) *An A-Z of reading and subject books,* NARE, from 4 Old Croft Road, Walton on the Hill Stafford.

Books for your children from 14 Stoke Road, Guildford, Surrey.

HART, J. and RICHARDSON, J. (1971) *Books for the retarded reader,* London, Ernest Benn.

LAWSON, K. S. (1968) *Children's reading,* Leeds Institute of Education, Pub. No. 8.

MOON, C. (1973) *Individualised reading,* Centre for Teaching Reading, University of Reading.

MUGFORD, L. (1970) *The Mugford readability chart* for assessing the difficulty of books, from L. Mugford, 14 The Park, Ealing, London, W5.

National Book League, *Help in reading,* 7 Albermarle St., London, W.1.

PASCOE, T. (1972) *Books for illiterate adults and adolescents,* available from the National Association for Remedial Education, or Association for Special Education,

PULLEN, A. (1962) *Words of persuasion,* Birmingham, Combridge Ltd.

ROOT, B. (1973) *Learning to read,* Centre for Teaching Reading, University of Reading.

APPENDIX 6

A selection of reading schemes and sets of books for less able pupils.

Approximate reading age ranges for most of these can be obtained from the sources listed in Appendix 5.

INFANT/LOWER JUNIOR LEVEL

Laugh and Learn series, Tom Stacey.
Royal Road Readers (first books), Chatto & Windus.
Early to Read & *Racing to Read*, E. J. Arnold.
Bangers and Mash, Bks. 1–14, Longman.
Language in Action, Macmillan.

JUNIOR LEVEL

Griffin Readers & *Dragon Stories*, E. J. Arnold.
Monster Books, Longman.
The Signal Books, Methuen.
Look Out Gang, Gibson.
Oxford Colour Reading Books (early stages), Oxford University Press
Sketetons 1–6, Longman.

JUNIOR/SECONDARY LEVEL

Tim's Gang Readers, six books, Hamish Hamilton.
Carford Readers, eight books, Pergamon Press.
Data Reading Scheme, Schofield & Sims.
*Club 75, various titles, Macmillan.
*Rescue Reading Series, Ginn & Co.
Story Path to Reading (2nd edition), Peter Leyden Pub. Co., Artarmon,
    N.S.W.

SECONDARY LEVEL

Inner Ring Series, (two series with 12 books each), Ernest Benn.
*Focus Books, six titles, Blackie & Son.
Crown Street Kings, Macmillan.
Popswingers Series, Hulton.
Stories for Today, Heinemann.
*Orbit Books, Macmillan
*Flag Series, Macmillan
*Patchwork Paperbacks, Cassell.
Read, Write and Enjoy, Oliver & Boyd.
Encounter series, Cassell.
Headlines, Edward Arnold.
Bulls Eye Books, Hutchinson.
Tempo Readers, Longman.
Instant Readers, Heinemann
*Joan Tate Readers, Heinemann.
*Jet Books, Cape.
*Trend Books, Ginn.
Spirals, Hutchinson.

*Particularly recommended for 'reluctant' readers.

APPENDIX 7

Sources for miscellaneous reading aids, games, machines, etc.

Audio-Page (Ricoh Synchrofax), E. J. Arnold, Butterley Street, Leeds LS10 1AX.

Autobates teaching machine, Autobates Ltd, Whitestone House, Lutterworth Road, Nuneaton.

Bingley Tutor (teaching machine), E. J. Arnold, Leeds.

Canterbury teaching machine, E.S.A. Harow, Essex.

Chip Club paperbacks, Scholastic Publications, 161 Fulham Road, London, SW3 6SW

English colour code programme for reading and spelling (D. Moseley), Senlac Systems Ltd, 351 Portobello Road, London, W10.

Film-strips, recordings and books, Weston-Woods Studio Ltd., 14 Friday Street, Henley-on-Thames, Oxon.

The Holt basic reading systems, London and New York, Holt Rinehart, & Winston.

King of the Road kit for adults with literacy problems. Oliver & Boyd, Edinburgh (obtainable from Longman Group Ltd, Pinnacles, Harlow, Essex).

Languagemaster (machine), Bell & Howell Ltd. Alperton House, Bridgewater Road, Wembley, Middlesex.

Pictogram reading system (L. Wendon), Pictogram Supplies, Barton, Cambridge.

Reading by rainbow (E. & W. Bleasdale), Moor Platt Press, Horwich, Lancs.

Reading routes, 120 individualised reading assignments, Longman Group Ltd, Harlow, Essex.

Reading workshops 6–10 and 9–13, Ward Lock Educational, 116 Baker Street, London W1M 2BB.

Scott-Foresman reading system, Scott-Foresman, 32 West Street, Brighton, BN1 2RT.

S.R.A. Laboratories (Reading, Listening, Language), S.R.A. Ltd. Reading Road, Henley on Thames, Oxon.

Stillitron teaching aid, Stillit Books Ltd., 72 New Bond Street, London W1.

Stott: *Programmed reading kit*, Holmes-McDougall Ltd, Allander House, Leith Walk, Edinburgh EH6 8NS.

Tapes, word games, card and worksheet materials, apparatus, Remedial Supply Co. Dixon Street, Wolverhampton.

The way to work, kit comprising career booklets, word bank, facsimile forms etc. for less able school leavers, Macmillan, Basingstoke.

The Webster classroom reading clinic (W. Kottmeyer), McGraw Hill, Maidenhead (and New York).

Wordmaster major game, Macdonald Educational, 72/90 Worship Street, London W1A.

Useful booklets and pamphlets (not free) on all aspects of reading and materials from: (i) Centre for Teaching Reading, 29 Eastern Avenue, Reading.

(ii) School Psychological Service of West Sussex, County Hall, Chichester.

APPENDIX 8

A selection of useful number/mathematics schemes, workcards, etc.

Arithmetic Readiness Cards Scott Foresman

Count and Colour and *Countdown,* Oliver & Boyd.

First mathematics, six books, Chapman.

First mathematics activity cards, Nelson.

Focus mathematics, Pergamon Press.

Four A Day/Ten A Day Metric, Oliver & Boyd

Fun with mathematics, Blackwell.

Ground-work mathematics cards, Macmillan.

Hesse Graded Workbooks 1–5, Longman

Inner ring maths, Ernest Benn.

Key Maths, Oliver & Boyd

Let's discover mathematics: Workshop 1, A & C. Black.

Let's explore mathematics, Black.

Let's think about mathematics, Nelson.

Living mathematics (metric & decimal), Cassell.

Making mathematics, Oxford University Press.

Making sure of maths, Holmes McDougall.

Mathematical games and activities for first school, Chatto & Windus.

Mathematics for schools, Level I (5–7yrs), Level II (7–12yrs), Addison-Wesley.

A natural approach to mathematics, Pergamon.

New Oxford mathematics workcards, Oxford University Press.

Number in mathematics, Macmillan.

Patterns of mathematics assignment cards, Longman.

183

Roots of Number, Sets 1–6, Cassell
Starting points, Schofield & Sims.
Topics in practical mathematics, Nelson.

APPENDIX 9

Suppliers of mathematics apparatus

E. J. Arnold, Butterley Street, Leeds 10.
Cuisenaire Co. Ltd, 40 Silver Street, Reading.
E.S.A., Pinnacles, Harlow, Essex.
Galt & Co., P.O. Box 10, Cheadle, Cheshire.
Invicta Plastics Ltd., Educational Aids Division, Oadby, Leicester.
Metric-Aids Ltd (Dryad), St. Mary's Mill, Leicester.
Philip & Tacey Ltd, North Way, Walworth Industrial Estate, Andover.
Taskmaster Ltd, Morris Road, Leicester.

INDEX

Achievement quotient, 17
Adaptive education, 2, 16, 28, 150, 154, 165
Adult illiterates, 68, 70, 112, 114, 116–7, 127, 130, 179
Apparatus, reading, 112, 114, 116, 120–4, 134, 181
number, 98, 139–46, 183
Articulation, 3, 33, 49, 67, 96, 134, 178
Arithmetic, 74–82, 97
tests, 76, 81
Attainment age, 13
Attainment tests, 12, 17–20, 22, 76–7, 82
Attention span, 3, 86, 94, 97
Auditory discrimination, 4, 30, 34, 47–8, 57, 59, 61, 67, 95, 133
Auditory memory, 31, 50, 59, 61, 96–7
Auditory perception, 40, 49, 61, 67, 119
Auditory training, 94–7, 111, 119

Banding, 158
Basic sight vocabulary, 48, 52, 59, 61, 109, 114, 118–9, 120, 122
Benton *Visual Retention Test*, 47
Blends, letter (*see also* Sound blending), 53, 57, 110, 116
Books for slow learners, 60, 113, 179–81
Breakthrough to literacy, 66, 90, 109, 115, 120–1, 123
Burt-Vernon *Graded Word Reading Test* norms, 176

Careers advice, 166
Case conferences, 165
Case studies, 59–62, 69–71
Colour coding for reading, 116, 132, 181
Compensatory education, 16, 150, 152
Comprehension, 15, 30, 41, 50, 53–4, 58, 122–5

Conservation of number, 77, 82–3, 97, 139
Context, 15, 60, 110
Co-ordination, 2, 3, 5, 7, 47, 92–4, 117, 135
Copying skill, 4, 8, 47, 91
Counselling, 62, 87, 110, 166
Creative writing, 64, 66, 128–9, 136
Crossed-laterality, 93
Cuisenaire Number Apparatus, 146, 183

Decoding (*see also* phonics), 22, 29, 46, 59, 124
Diagnosis, 12, 14, 21, 24, 36, 39–58, 64, 68, 76–82
Diagnostic flow-diagram for reading, 44–5
teaching, 24, 84, 150, 154
Dictation, 60, 119, 122, 133, 143
Differential diagnosis, 84
Digraphs, 21, 53, 57, 59, 68, 114, 119
Dysgraphia, 67
Dyslexia, 67, 84

Early detection of difficulties, 1–8, 152
Encoding, 22, 29
English Proficiency Tests (N.F.E.R.), 37
E.P.V.T., 18, 29
Error analysis, 41, 54–7, 68, 72
Expressive language, 101
assessment of, 33–7, 40
training of, 102–6

Fernald remedial approach, 115, 134
First Grade Screening Test, 5
Flashcards, 62, 87, 91, 109, 111, 115, 118, 122, 133
Flying Start Kit, 94
Formboards, 3, 90
Form filling, 128–9